Barbara Masekela

Poli Poli

Barbara Masekela

JONATHAN BALL PUBLISHERS
Johannesburg • Cape Town • London

Originally published in South Africa in 2021 by
JONATHAN BALL PUBLISHERS
A division of Media24 (Pty) Ltd
PO Box 33977
Jeppestown
2043

ISBN 978-1-77619-095-9
ebook ISBN 978-1-77619-096-6

Every effort has been made to trace the copyright holders and to obtain their permission for the use of copyright material. The publishers apologise for any errors or omissions and would be grateful to be notified of any corrections that should be incorporated in future editions of this book.

www.jonathanball.co.za
www.twitter.com/JonathanBallPub
www.facebook.com/JonathanBallPublishers

Cover by Michiel Botha
Cover image by Brett Rubin
Childhood photograph provided by the author
Design and typesetting by Martine Barker
Printed and bound by CTP Printers, Cape Town
Set in Bembo Std/Agenda

For Minkie, aka Hugh

CONTENTS

ONE

THE PLACE OF KNEELING

THE ONLY home I knew was number 76 Witbank Location. We called it KwaGuqa – the Place of Kneeling. I lived there with my grandmother, Ouma Johanna Mabena Bower. I called her Ouma then, but over the next twenty-seven years she became Johanna, Jwana, Joey and Jwi as the locked doors opened and understanding replaced pure sentiment.

Born on 18 July 1941, I was the eldest daughter and the second child, and always to be preceded by my brother, who was two years older than me and called Minkie. His nickname was after the cartoon character Mickey Mouse. My ouma was almost five feet tall, her strong back perfectly straight except for her curved seat on which we rested as babies, tightly wrapped, our legs and arms embracing her. It would be six years before my sister, Elaine, was born. She came to KwaGuqa after she was weaned from the breast at nine months, as was the family custom.

My parents, then both employed in Alexandra, bought a state-of-the-art baby stroller for her with disastrous results. She would simply not have the safety belts strapped around her. Efforts to set the thing in motion put her into such a hysterical state that finally Ouma gave in and the stroller project was abandoned. '*Nee, nee, angifuni!*' (No, no, I don't want!) Nothing would make her ride in the stroller. She would not be coaxed or threatened. Eventually Ouma had to admit defeat and the stroller was folded and stored on top of the wardrobe. That was the end of the matter and Elaine was free to roam around the house and the yard, the dreaded stroller gone and never mentioned again.

She was a swift runner, and the quiet tenor of our life with Ouma was dominated by our race to keep up with her movements around the house and the yard. Her nickname became uMthubathubi – Speedy, now here, then there, like a sudden wind, in and out and everywhere, roughly translated – just as mine would be uMdzwayidzwayi, denoting a gangling spectre, head high up in the air, witness to everything.

In isiNdebele these names were pure poetic imagery, capturing pace, posture, gesture and repeated sound. This onomatopoeic quality in our everyday speech contained an element of a gentle humour that set the subject apart as someone special beyond their formal name. Indeed, I grew long-limbed and taller than my older brother as well as Ouma, who, despite her short stature, had the strength of a lion.

I follow Ouma's swift march to the gate and, with a momentary pause, she stops to pull out a weed from the flower bed along the side wall of our house and flicks the soil off her fingers. At the gate she halts, peering up and down the street. Now I can hear my Ouma's voice calling out for him, Mousieeeeee, Mousieeeeeee.

Her voice rises on the last syllable, elongating softly till the end of her breath. The call, unanswered, turns into a shriek and then the rant begins.

'This child is wild. He is *goddeloos* (godless). He comes, eats, sleeps, and then he is gone. A person cannot even have a conversation with him.' She speaks in Afrikaans, our home language, except when my cousins come to play, when we speak isiNdebele.

During the day we are always alone in the house and I have grown accustomed to the conversations she has with herself. When she asks, 'Jwana, where did you put the pair of scissors?' I run to the bedroom, get them from the dressing table and race to hand them to her. She smiles and thanks me: '*Dankie, my kind.*' (Thank you, my child.) I have learnt how to please her by anticipating my small chores, like throwing the chicken feed through the wide holes of their pen and watching the hens fly down from the open shelves where they lay eggs. It is my job to keep the saucer for our cat without a name clean and to fill it up with milk in the morning and water during the day. At this stage I also dust the furniture in the front room and seasonally I help to apply Brasso to the big squat orb vase on the sideboard in the front room, before she polishes it with the yellow duster until it gleams. I follow her around the house picking up this, taking that there and helping her tidy up. The drawer of the dressing table in our bedroom is massed with miscellaneous medicines, Aspro, Zam-Buk ointment, milk of magnesia, Epsom salts, castor oil, a big Vaseline bottle, and tiny brown bottles of Boere medicines like *duiwelsdrek, haarlemensis, rooi laventel, witdulsies* and *doepa.*

We live by ourselves in the four-roomed house with a high veranda in the front and a backyard with a rectangular chicken coop on the distant side of the back fence and the water closet with a puller chain that flushes with a loud whoosh gradually changing into distinct gurgle followed by a diminishing hum. Our toilet paper is old newspapers. We tear a piece, crush it and then softly rub it with both hands to soften it before use. Minkie lives with our parents and comes to visit on school holidays from Payneville, a model African location in Springs. As in the other townships in nearby Brakpan, Benoni and Boksburg, the dwellers are officially called non-white or non-European. But by 1950 these townships, close to the towns, with one main street, will each be declared a 'black spot' under the Group Areas Act. The inhabitants will be classified into ethnic groups and formally separated from their Asian neighbours, and an in-between group of mixed-race people will be reinforced to serve as a boom gate to keep Africans even further away from 'Europeans'.

At seven years old Minkie leaves KwaGuqa to live in City Deep, where my father is employed as a mine clerk and studies privately to qualify as one of the first black health inspectors in South Africa. With him they move to Payneville, where, in his new post, he motivates for the establishment of a fresh produce market and milk depot. Years earlier, my mother, newly married and unemployed, has the chance to advance herself through the Jan H Hofmeyr School of Social Work. Opened in 1941 in Johannesburg, it offers a new channel of professional training for Africans. Its graduates include Ellen Khuzwayo and Joshua Nkomo, among many notable black professionals. Conveniently located in the city, it also offers urban black people the opportunity to commute from home. It is the perfect option for further education for my mother. Though my father cannot afford to pay the fees, he agrees that she should further her studies. My mother appeals to Ouma to assist her and, with my father's agreement, Ouma commits to paying the fees and to helping to look after me while my mother is studying. That is how I came to live in KwaGuqa from the time I was nine months old.

Our favourite relative at the time is my beautiful Auntie Tinnie, who calls my mother Sis Pannie. She is the youngest daughter of Ouma's older sister, whom we call Ouma Sussie. She is always in trouble about school and other matters I am not allowed to know about. I am not allowed to ask questions about her comings and goings. In between her troubles she lives with my mother and father and once she is even sent to the Talitha Home for Non-European Girls in Johannesburg, an 'experiment in the field of Juvenile Delinquency' led by white missionary women to 'armour' black girls to 'meet the problems and allurements of life in an urban community', according to the home's 1937 report. Everybody is seized with her escapades. Her saving grace is that she is hardworking, humorous and very handy around the house. In particular, it is her love of jiving that gets her into trouble. When there is a visiting band from Johannesburg my parents refuse her permission to go to the dance hall. She jumps out of the window when everyone is asleep. It is Minkie, her accomplice, who waits and, half-asleep, listens for the knock at the window to let her back in while everybody sleeps. For now, Minkie is here on December school holidays. Auntie Tinnie lives with him and my parents in Payneville. She has been on good behaviour and attends night school. They hope she can finish her JC (Junior Certificate) and go for nurses' training.

Like her, Minkie is always in trouble. He roams around KwaGuqa with my cousins Gigigi and Fani, and beyond the authorised boundaries, and into forbidden veld where the Boer farmers live with their hunting dogs and their guns and their flower gardens and their perfectly symmetrical fields verdant with maize and vegetables and orchards.

The Boer men shoot guns in the air to frighten off intrepid black boys in search of adventure. The boys sneak under the wire fences of the Boer farms and feast on the mulberries, peaches and apricots. We have no clue that our grandmothers have intimate knowledge of shooting rifles and bomb explosions, or that they are familiar with spurting human blood. They do not tell us. They scold, a lot. We do not know what they mean when they say, 'It is enough now. Enough blood has been shed.'

I have heard Ouma and her Sussie talk in whispers about a time long ago, even before my mother was born. I am only seven years old and unable to follow all the shifts of the conversation, which are matched with laughter, sudden silences, much nose-blowing and wiping of eyes.

All I can understand is that I was not there. They were young on the farm and mostly they talk about dead people. They chortle about their favourite uncle who was a composer of instant hit songs. The two sisters prod each other's memories searching for a song, but first they paint a pastoral scene of a rest day away from the fields and the white farm owners' household. Then Ouma Sussie, with a strong contralto, re-enacts his performance of the song about Maria, their aunt, an expert brewer of traditional beer. He sang of her futile activity, warning that all her efforts were in vain because, 'All, all of the people, all the people, will be gone. No one will be there to drink your beer.'

The chorus is the only fragment of the lyrics that will not leave me alone. It echoes inside my head and I search with no success for the isiNdebele words that come before the refrain. But the voices of my granny sisters still ring in my ears. I see them now, in rhythm, each putting her hands together without a sound but in time with the other, their palms parting and meeting in time, without the clap.

'NoMaaaaria,' they call out in song. And then they stop with a chuckle and pull their faces back into this moment. They reach for the hems of their *voorskote* (aprons). Ouma Sussie makes as if to get up, straightening her back and stretching one leg after the other. My Ouma, Johanna, gets up from the bench they are sharing in the shade of the apricot tree, then sits down again and calls out for me to get her snuff. I bring the snuffbox and some bush tea with milk and sugar and hear them saying, 'Lydenburg is where this one went and that one may still be in Barberton. They say he was last heard of in Kimberley. Indeed, all the people have gone. It is only us, left here in KwaGuqa.' They do this often, speaking to each other as though I am not there with them.

One or the other will begin to speak again. 'Do you still remember So-and-So?' One Alpheus, or Jacobus, or Johannes. 'The one who was the eldest son of the Skhosanas? No, he was a Mahlangu, related to us by the marriage between our small father Andries and the Monnakgotla woman? They were Tswana.' And so they carry on, correcting each other, nudging each other's memories. A cousin, a neighbour, an uncle – all gone and disappeared on some farm in Bronkhorstspruit or Delmas, one last seen on his way to get a job on the mines in Germiston and the father drowned on the seas with the *SS Mendi*. Or that one who never returned after signing up for the Native Labour Corps in the Great War.

Ja, the ones who returned came back and were rewarded with bicycles.

But the white men got medals!

Public parades were organised for them.

White veterans indeed!

Settled in special houses with running water and electricity.

Given jobs on the railways and in the offices in the municipalities.

Some of them could hardly read or write.

But we had to call them *baas* because they controlled the passes.

Ruefully, Ouma remarks, '*Nee, wit mense is 'n ander nasie!*' (Whites are of another type of people!) It was all just a matter-of-fact cataloguing, a resigned recapitulation to say that this is the shape of the world as we know it, a plaint maybe.

My memories of childhood are of women in black. Picking up on scraps of their conversations, it seems that men disappear or die and women mourn and carry on. In my KwaGuqa family there are no grandfathers, only those sepia portraits of dead old men in severe Victorian suits caught by the cameras in a moment of ramrod posture with their unsmiling brides with distant looks. Their expressions symbolise the lot of women. They all look straight ahead. Ouma's husband, Walter Bower, died in 1938, the year my mother, Pauline Elizabeth Bower, married my father, Thomas Selema Masekela. A white South African of Scottish origin, Walter Bower stands elegant, stiff, thin-lipped with a moustache, in the wedding picture that hangs in Ouma's *voorkamer* (front room) next to their framed marriage certificate. These commemorations stand in for his absence in the lives of Ouma, my mother and my Uncle Bower. And when she heard of his death in the house of his mistress, a coloured woman who also ran a tavern on Sivewright Avenue, in Doornfontein, she took out her marriage certificate and boarded the train to Johannesburg to go to court and claim his dead body for burial here in KwaGuqa.

The shifts in my grannies' reminiscences always point back in the direction of the Lutheran mission station in Middelburg. 'Merensky! Eiselen!' they exclaim repeatedly, still incredulous about the cold discipline, the hardness of heart coupled with the devout service to the Almighty. It is as though they still cannot believe these events have taken place, and it seems that, in repeating them, they are still putting together a puzzle with some of the pieces missing.

In time, towards sunset, Minkie slinks home with his clothes splotched with mulberry stains, his khaki shorts ripped in places and stained with blood from barbed-wire fence cuts.

Later, after the hiding with the belt, after the howling, the pleading and the promising not to do it again, after her shouting in time to the blows, Ouma hums another nameless song carrying out her chores. I love my brother. He is sitting alone behind the coal shed. I go there and I say, '*Askies*, Minkie.' (I'm sorry, Minkie.)

I can still smell the cooked dumplings risen over the beef stew and hear the rattling of the yellow enamel plates as she prepares to dish up our supper. Minkie, the hiding forgotten, regales me with tales about the chase, how the fat farmer set his dogs on them, how they outran the man and his dogs, crept under the fence, the sound of rifle bullets zinging in their ears, their eyes almost blinded by the dust kicked up by the bullets. Breathless with anticipation and admiration mixed with envy, I drink in the fantastical tale: '*En toe?*' (And then?)

It is Tinnie who interrupts my 'And then?' Always bustling around, tidying up or finishing up the ironing. Auntie Tinnie is like a balm. She is full of life, as my mother says. She knows all about bands and films, and recounts nightly the story in *Sentimental Journey* when we cuddle up to her on the bed we all share. She is obsessed with the film and soon I too am sucked into the tale of the little girl who loses her adoptive mother and strives to win the love of her grieving father, who will not be consoled. The dead mother regularly appears to the child as a ghost and becomes the link between the dead woman and the grieving widower. Auntie Tinnie sings the song from the film incessantly and soon it becomes my song too. Like most popular hit songs from Hollywood films, it captures our imagination although we do not always fully understand the true meaning of the lyrics. But I regularly parrot the words, 'Gonna take a sentimental journey.' I mumble most of the words, but for some reason I seize on the multisyllabic words, raising my voice in emphasis when I get to 'sentimental', 'reservation' and 'anticipation'. For some strange reason I cannot understand, Ouma is soon irritated by my constant singing of the song and my aunt is severely reprimanded for teaching me about things children should not be allowed to know. So, I hum the song softly when she is not within earshot. My Auntie Tinnie wears 4711 scent like my mother and it seems she is always getting ready to go somewhere.

She is also the kind one, the one who will interrupt my brother's tall stories, '*Hayi suka Minkie. Yek' ukukhohlisa umtwana!*' (Stop deceiving the child!)

On another occasion my brother comes home ash-grey, his clothes damp and smelly from swimming in the dam with the coal-black water from the mine. The hidings with the belt have become another game for him. I listen with horror at the blows falling. But now he is so foxy he dodges them, and once even dives between Ouma's legs and slips through to her back, so that she nearly falls trying to aim another blow, her legs akimbo. It is to Ouma Sussie's house that he runs.

Under the tree in her long, black robes sits my Ouma Kappie, our great-grandmother, the only person in the world whom Ouma cannot defy. The one who calls her Jwana, who commands her to sit down and shut up, who says to her, 'If you touch him, then you have to deal with me ...'

The tale of his misdeeds is reported in detail to my mother when she comes to take him back at the end of the holidays. Ouma is irritated by my mother's reaction, which is always calm and conciliatory. She asks Minkie, 'Didn't I tell you not to worry Ouma? Go to her now and apologise, at once, you naughty boy.'

Ouma snorts, 'How you spoil the child! *No* good is going to come of this spoiling.' And that is the end of it.

It is my mother's way, always, to calm things down and Minkie, her first child and a boy to boot, is the apple of her eye. Together, they are apart from the attention my father showers on me.

On one occasion Ouma and I have to take a sudden visit to Springs. We find Mama in bed with her eye bandaged. I am told she has had to have an eye operation. My aunt is there from Lichtenburg and that night there is a big family conference and

Minkie and I are sent to bed. All I can hear is Ouma saying something about, 'You promised not to raise your hand again,' just before I fall asleep. The following day we return to KwaGuqa. Still in her late twenties, my mother is alight with smiles and entertaining ideas and when she is in a room there are a million tiny bells that sound joyfully. I am struck by how everyone wants to have a conversation with her so that I cannot have her to myself. Her short visits pass quickly and before I know it she has to leave me again. I sit on her lap and at night I wait in bed for her so that I can lay my head close to her bosom. No one else is ever that close to me.

In KwaGuqa she is called Pannie, but Minkie and I address her as Mama Atshi. It is Ouma's special name for her. Boyboy is another of my mother's names for Minkie. They are tight. He takes piano lessons now and everyone thinks he is a genius. Those two, my ouma sometimes says, are more like brother and sister. Besides, hadn't my father rushed into the house in Payneville when he heard both of them screaming with terror? He found them standing on the table, their arms around each other. They had just seen a mouse scampering and sniffing around the kitchen floor.

Uncle Kenny never tires of telling the story of a Sunday afternoon in Payneville. The adults were in the kitchen with some friends, regaling each other with stories from the past, and Minkie was playing in his room with his newest toy, a fire engine that Kenny had bought for him. He was going up and down to the kitchen, filling a cup with water. On his third relay my uncle's suspicion was roused and he decided to peek into the room. Flames were rising up the curtain and my brother was extinguishing the fire with the cups of water! That is Minkie, always managing to endear himself – even when he courts danger.

✥ ✥ ✥

THE BLUR of my early childhood is punctuated by raised voices between Ouma and her son Khalo, my uncle – Uncle Bower.

Although my recollection of that time is patchy it is the shouting and screaming between Khalo and Ouma that dominates, and the name Tillie, sung out by the son and spat out by the mother. There is soot and blood on ripped clothes; the groans and growls, between blows, pushing and heaving towards the coal bin, rising and falling, are all punctuated with the name Tillie, spat out, cried out and sobbed. Tillie! Tillie! It is always about Tillie, Khalo's girlfriend, Mira's daughter from the rambunctious shebeen a few doors away.

This is big trouble. I am helpless without Minkie. Ouma and Khalo seem tethered together in a wrestling hold. I must find my brother. He will help. I run, run, run to the gate. The plants are still wet with the early morning dew but he is already playing in the street. 'Minkie! Minkie, *kom, kom*.' He hears, he comes, he sees, and he runs to Ouma Sussie's.

He follows me, takes one look and flies to Ouma Sussie's house for help, and then all the Mtswenis are there: Uncle Putukwana, Auntie Tinnie, my cousin Wincie. I am there, pulling on Ouma's skirts. There they find us as if posing for a photograph. I am sobbing next to my ouma, who is sitting, legs stretched out, leaning on the coalshed wall, Khalo lying on her other side, holding his mother's hand with her thumb bleeding and dangling down. The neighbours from both sides of our house are there too and for a while everything is paused. I can't remember anything more.

In the ensuing commotion someone gets onto his bicycle to call for the police to come and Uncle Khalo is taken away. The rest is a blank, but for the rest of my life I understand the word 'ruction'. It is one of the words Ouma uses when our clients raise their voices at each other. I understand now why she always says, 'I want no ruction in my house!' I now become a silent *mdzwayidzwayi*, wishing to be unseen and unheard but watchful and quiet, bereft of speech for a few days until my mother arrives and takes me away. No one ever speaks again of the incident. But it sticks in the back of my mind, forever on replay.

I learn from eavesdropping that my uncle has been committed to a hospital for mad people. Six months later, he is released with Ouma's intervention and that of a lawyer paid for by her. When I read a letter my mother has written to Ouma, I learn he has been discharged from the mental institution and is living and working in Brakpan at a butchery. He is repentant and wants to reconcile with Ouma. After the bandages are removed from her hand, her thumb emerges pale, pink and always pointing towards her. Every day I see her disfigured thumb and on occasion I catch her exercising it, massaging it away to lie down across her palm.

Like most of the black men born in Witbank, Khalo seeks refuge far away from KwaGuqa and cuts himself off from us. His fight with Ouma has freed him to leave. It is a closed subject. I know too that I must never refer to it. It is only when she prays at night that I know he is always on her mind and that she would do anything to have him back in KwaGuqa. Minkie, my authority on worldly matters, is also silent about this issue, so I let it go. I am always guarded and even at Ouma Sussie's house, where there is much more laxity, I am careful not to say too much about Ouma's business. But I bask in Ouma Sussie's affectionate attention, especially because I realise that my mother shares certain confidences with her. When they think I am out of earshot they speak about Ouma's unnecessary strictness and they laugh kindly about her. It seems to me that I am always to be a keeper of certain secrets and I begin to learn that not everything has to be blurted out, that trust means care and subtlety.

For instance, I notice that there are times when my granny sisters are not speaking to each other, but I am never forbidden from going to Ouma Sussie's house. Hers is the only house where I am permitted to eat and to play, and, after a few weeks of a stand-off, she walks down the street to break the silence.

'Jwi, this cannot continue,' she starts as she enters the kitchen door, leaning heavily on her wooden cane.

Jwi was the fondest name she called Ouma and she was the only one who addressed her like that. With 'Jwi', She could always break the silence.

We were taught to greet the neighbours and to accord them the respect due to all our elders, but we were hardly familiar with the inside of their homes. Ouma's regard for them was based solely on the condition of their laundry on the *draad* (clothes line) and how early the smoke rose from their chimneys, how the glass on their windows glittered with the reflection of the bright sun and the shimmer of red polish on their stoep.

❖❖❖

KWAGUQA, where we kneel. People say the name with a resigned flourish, exaggerating the click on the last syllable, their tongue on the palate, with a small smile and an exclamation mark. It is as if saying 'KwaGuqa' out aloud evokes other places and other times, from which we are now excluded. Yet, in a strange way, where they had been before is always with us. Overhearing random stories they tell and retell one another, we catch them looking over their shoulders to make sure we are not catching the slip of their tongues. They clear their throats and pitch their voices, recalling happy times, singing ditties of '*wit gepoeier maar nie hare nie*' (powdered all white, but no hair to show) or imitating festive Dutch people dancing to 'Jan Pierewiet' or

'Bokkie, ons gaan nie huis toe' (Bokkie, we're not going home). We sense that, in these moments, they are in a faraway place that we will never know, very near to where they came from. We don't feature in this picture, unless they ask us to bring the Lutheran Sepedi hymn book and we sing lustily with them, *'O nkishe Jesu Krestu mo o eang teng'* (Oh lead me, Jesus Christ, wherever you are going). We are like passengers in a vehicle with an unknown destination we have not chosen.

Soon the setting sun remarks on their stolen leisure, reminding them to shout out orders for the coal bin to be filled or the water to be heated for the evening ablutions. We can tell that before KwaGuqa there had been other places they had had to leave unexpectedly, that they had carried pots and pans and dishes and blankets and brooms and chairs from place to place in the dark and sometimes with the rain mixing with their tears.

They did not choose KwaGuqa but they could neither turn back nor go further to find some other place. This is where they can now be at peace. They have come to know it best, not because it is better but because it is there. Here they will never again have fields of their own to cultivate and they will never again have the pleasure of counting cows and pigs and sheep or filling bags with peaches and apricots, or gathering eggs in baskets to sell. But here they have some certainty of waking up in their own beds, here they will not have to watch the covetous gaze of jealous bigots unashamed to reap what they have not sown. They own very little but what they now have is theirs. They are free from the continuous inspection of the keen rural masters, themselves just rescued from rabid poverty. Here they will never again be on the road to the unknown or hear the order, 'Off my land by the time the sun rises.' No longer tenant farmers or sharecroppers, they rest awhile in KwaGuqa Native Location, and every day they kneel. They kneel, weary from worry about the ones left behind, the ones paying rent to farm the land that was once their own, and those paying with three months' labour so that they can continue to stay on the land – their land. They stayed behind, in every way.

We, too, like children everywhere, are fascinated by the notion that they have ever been young and we can't imagine that once upon a time their grandfathers owned land. We cannot grasp the idea of their being descended from kings and other nobility because they have nothing to show for it. Everything about KwaGuqa refutes the past we overhear them describing. It makes nonsense of their long, long ago cameos told in swiftly edited, disjointed episodes. Rather, we memorise Hans Christian Andersen's fairy tales and imagine ourselves wearing glass slippers with no thought of how hard, cold and impractical they would be for walking. Theirs is not nostalgia but a glancing reminder of the unspeakable, and they tuck it away where, unseen, it ferments and can only be stilled by the promise of our young lives. We are mixed up in the schooling that they advocate and wearied by repeatedly told stories of the Lutheran missionaries who taught them how to become religious domestic servants. By their own admission, they distrust the word of the white man.

'Look what they did in 1910,' they shrug.

And someone else retorts, 'What about 1913?'

And then there is a babble of angry voices stilled by a temporary impotence.

We are children. We are driven by them to acquire that which has eluded them even as new rumours of difficult times ahead swirl and dizzy our minds. Our history books show only lithographs of white men with flags and stern faces, dressed in full European regalia, blousy shirts, pants and decorated jackets. In the illustrations of school texts, the white men stand on the sterns of hulky ships with names we have to commit to memory. They survey the land beyond the angry rocky Cape ocean. In the background of the pictures there are indistinct figures of inscrutable half-naked men, women and children dressed in loinskins, carrying small pouches of arrows, wandering around in isolation, drifters in search of roots, wild fruits and beasts to kill with their poisoned arrows. In my white shirt and black gym dress with block pleats, these figures do not inspire feelings of kinship within me, I feel no connection to them.

Still, some teachers like that young male teacher at my Anglican school at KwaGuqa will, for a while, set aside the official textbook and tell us stories about the wisdom of great, dead, old men, kings like Moshoeshoe, Sekhukhune, Mabhogo, Hintsa, Sobhuza and many others who ruled with sagacity against the white tide that drenched the land and forced them on a continuous trek to wars and battles they had not declared. He says it has not always been the rule that we are without power. He says that one day we will rise again to take back what is ours. He says we need to distinguish between what we need to know in order to pass examinations and what we need to hold fast to so we can change life as we know it. Although he does not vow us to secrecy, we know that this is something we should keep close to our chests so that it always remains new. And it does.

At KwaGuqa, we kneel to bury the sealed four-gallon tin of yeast, leavened and brewed in the veld above the location. The brew in the *mgogogos* (tins) is covered with earth and ripened in the sun-warmed holes. No brewer, having staked out her area, ever intrudes on another's territory. Routinely it is my Ouma Johanna who kneels in the veld at dusk because she cannot afford the price of hole diggers, *izembamgodi*.

We kneel to pray at night. I ask that the mud from the rain not seep into the buried tins and spoil the beer. We cannot keep the beer to mature in the house for fear that there might be a police raid. That is why Ouma has to kneel again and again in the open veld, whether it rains and thunders, or in the dusky winter evenings when the sun seems to dip down too quickly and the wind turns icy. She must kneel to remove the camouflage, to lift out the heavy tin. She must kneel so that my mother can finish school, she must kneel so that we can eat.

The *izembamgodi* occupy the lowest position in the small industry. In some home taverns they fulfil all the roles, from digging the holes to buying the ingredients, brewing the liquor, serving the customers, recruiting new clients, cleaning and clearing up at the end of the day. Not least, they spy on rival businesses and keep a watch for police on an unexpected raid. For all of this they might be provided with a sleeping place and some food. But mainly, they sponge off the clients for free drinks. In the event of a raid, they are arrested in place of the tavern owner, a main reason for their employment. Most of the drinking places are run by older homeowners, women who have chosen not to do domestic work in the homes of the newly promoted poor whites who live and work as petty officials for the new apartheid government in Witbank.

✦ ✦ ✦

OUMA'S STRICT rules to uphold her tavern as a decent place with no ructions mean there is no loud talking, singing, dancing or fighting allowed. Indeed, there are certain ruffians who are not admitted across the threshold of our tavern. We have no radio or gramophone and I have no stories to match those of my peers who witness all kinds of dramas at their tavern homes. There is no formal association of beer brewers. It is a small coterie of women who still specialise in authentic African beer with wholesome, nourishing ingredients. Outside of this small group there are others who make mind-bending concoctions and also sell European liquor. They work hand in hand with bottle-store workers and enterprising policemen as well as certain white men who want to make money on the side. Ouma is well known for the limits she places on those who enter number 76, and even the hole diggers preferred not to work for her – except for Auntie Tsiri, who is a Mabena and a relative. Tsiri lives wherever she finds herself in the morning but her home is at the Tollmans', where she is an adopted distant relative. Their house is around the corner from Ouma Sussie's.

Auntie Tsiri's complexion is a vivid brown, with splotches of dark brown on her high cheeks, like flames dying. Her mouth is always slightly open, her inner lower lip brightly pink. She has what is called a *phuza* face (drink face). Her calloused hands tremble as she fumbles to find a handkerchief in the half-moon-shaped pocket of her blue German-print *voorskoot*, now a faded grey.

'Drink some water,' Ouma is always telling her, 'and make yourself some tea and bread.'

My Ouma is in her late fifties and by all standards an old woman in my mind. When Ouma needs help, she sends me to look for Tsiri, who scrubs the linoleum floor and then prepares the utensils for sieving the brew before she walks with Ouma to unearth two tins of the liquor at dusk. Each with a four-gallon tin carried on her head, they half-trot back to the house without spilling a drop. When Tsiri can't be found, Ouma does the trip twice by herself. Always in tow, I witness how, in one swoop, she lifts the four-gallon tin and balances it on her head and in a half-run carries it to our house. She kneels in the corner of the kitchen and unties the rope around the layers of hessian sacks laden with damp soil that clothe the tin. Kneeling still, she uncovers the tin to see the race of instant bubbles spawning in the pungent smell of the fermented yeast, and breathes in the drunken aroma that earns us our livelihood.

There are all kinds of variations to make the liquor – the 'kaffir beer', as the authorities call it – more potent by adding potatoes, pineapple and what are said to be traditional herbs rumoured to make the clients come back for more. On the Gold Reef, a variety called *sibapana le masenke* causes the drinkers to cling to the zinc of the shack walls for balance. Ouma prides herself on her brew, always made with malt, yeast and brown sugar, on which her clients get tipsy but can always walk home. Tsiri leaves the house after her duties because Ouma does not allow women to mix with her clients. She allows no carousing in her *ordentlike* (decent) house.

It is only Mira, now living in drunken penury, three houses from number 76, who has the reputation of having run a roaringly successful speakeasy, like the ones shown in bioscope pictures seen on visits to the big cities. I can't believe that the ruin that is Mira's house now once had singing and jiving, with men sitting on sofas and some in a private room reserved for the occasional white man, including some policemen who were frequent clients. He is Tillie's father and Ouma's sworn enemy, just like Ouma Martha on the corner of the street on the way to the Anglican church, who holds the status of pariah because even the white policemen drink at her beautiful house with a decorated iron gate at the bottom of the steps leading to her lavish front room that few KwaGuqa residents have ever entered.

Once in a while Ouma takes my hand to go and check if our things (*onse goede*) in the veld are safe. It is usually when she has had an ominous dream the night before. We trudge through the green grass, sometimes up to her waist. This is where she teaches me to pull out the stalks of the long grass and suck their delicate, sweet nectar. She also shows me the clumps of purple flowers that grow close to the ground. We gather them and stuff them into our apron pockets before she puts them in a bowl of water when we get home. We rub them together in our palms and with the generous lather comes a fragrant scent. I am fascinated. She explains that they used these flowers to wash before they learnt how to make their own soap at the mission school.

At times the horn of the chugging goods train on its way to the Reef and to Mozambique startles my kneeling ouma, deep in thought over whether she can continue to pay my mother's fees at the Jan H Hofmeyr School of Social Work and put food in my mouth also. I remember this when I rub her back with Zam-Buk. My small fists pummel the sorest parts and I feel grown-up, like Auntie Tinnie, who sometimes massages Ouma's sore back. The long history of her back is a story Ouma repeatedly tells and I know it by heart. For once I do not carry sole culpability for her pains. She has carried water and firewood balanced on her head from childhood, carried babies of her own on this back, my aunts and my uncles, then Minkie and me.

The mining houses brew their own liquor to stop their labourers from drinking in the location houses. But the labourers still choose to drink in the houses of the old women, away from the workplace. Most of these labourers are from other lands too far away to imagine; they hate the mine hostels, where they are crowded with no privacy and sleep on concrete bunk beds with only a curtain to separate them from one another. They do not have warmth from a low burning coal stove or enjoy the linger-ing whiff of fried onions, tomatoes, ground peanuts and *morogo* (wild spinach). They say wistfully how their sons and daughters, who were mere babies when they left, must be 'this high' now, gesturing with crooked arm, 'He must be talking by now.' They remark on the contours of the female shapes they see at the mine hostel gates and on the streets who look 'just like my wife'. They forget themselves and go into the detail of soft, curved bosoms until Ouma crows, 'Enough, I am raising a child in this house.'

Ouma is a strong, practical innkeeper who doesn't hesitate to drag a grown man out of her kitchen, to the gate and over into the street if the house rules are broken. I am responsible for collecting payments and providing the change. After the men leave we count the money together and I separate it into shillings, sixpences, tickeys and pennies and tie it up in handkerchiefs. Ouma's efforts to run a decent house include a draughts board. Our customers play the game avidly and I have become the reigning champion and await the arrival of the men eagerly at the end of the day.

After one of his visits, my father quickly puts an end to my pleasant pastime. He does not think it right that an eight-year-old girl should engage in such activity with drinking men. My father doesn't register a single complaint to Ouma. Rather, Mama is the messenger. It is a cause for much tension, but Ouma finally relents while grumbling that it is the liquor she sells that is educating the very daughter who married into the Masekela family.

✢ ✢ ✢

KWAGUQA IS sometimes a dangerous place. White men in long leather boots jump out of olive-green sidecars and surprise us out of our sleep. They burst into the rooms without knocking, overturning the chamber pot as they look under the beds, shouting, 'Where is it? Where is it?' They pull open the wardrobe doors and fling our clothes onto the floor, trampling all over our Sunday best. Ouma in her long flannel nightdress faces them with feigned indignation. All the tools of her trade have been washed clean the night before and there is not a scintilla of evidence to be found at number 76. She was warned that there would be a raid three days ago already. One of the gardeners, while clearing the flower bed under the window at the charge office, overheard the officers plotting the raid during their tea break.

With word of a raid, my grandmother makes a quick visit to her sister, Ouma Sussie, at her corner house at the top of our street. Such intelligence means that we have to suspend our business for a while. Those evenings are quiet without the cheer of the men from the mines, who are our customers. The old women grimly empty the four gallon tins of beer down the drain, cursing the dogs who are taking the food from our mouths. But there is also the joy of gloat each time they outfox the police. So we learn early that there are good lies and bad lies.

We know that the menu for the following days will be *morogo* and pap until the danger of arrest has passed and we can once more collect the pennies, tickeys and sixpences, the shillings and the five bobs, to buy meat again. We wait for the dawn when the booted ones rattle on doors and windows, cursing and shouting, 'Open up or we'll break down the blerrie door!' And our grannies relish the discomfiture on the faces of the policemen, who leave with neither evidence nor prisoners.

They are always prepared for the uncertainty of whatever it is that may come. It causes them to worry about how they would feed us. But it also changes our routine. It is the only time we can go with Ouma to spend time at Ouma Sussie or Oupa Jacobus, her brother who lives in the next street with his wife Ouma Planka, who is named by us after the wooden planks on her covered veranda floor. Their grandson Gigigi is Minkie's best friend. We enjoy seeing them together, talking about the whereabouts of lost relatives and the news in the letters from their children. All my maternal aunts and uncles are living on the mines on the Reef, in the 'native compounds'.

It is fun hearing them sing hymns in Sepedi or breaking into old isiNdebele wedding songs. They make loud remarks about our behaviour in our full hearing and we feign agreement with their spontaneous judgement of how we will turn out in the future. They each drink a tot of brandy from a small bottle, like a toy, which they call a nip or *ismehlane*. The nearest size to a full bottle is a bigger bottle they call a half-jack. But before that they offer a libation to the ancestors. It is a strict ritual to pour a small amount of whatever they are going to drink onto the ground in a corner of the room or at the threshold of the door before they take a single sip. We don't ask them how the departed spirits can quench their thirst from the ground but, like our grannies, we trust that the ancestors will shield us from the unknown. At about 8:30 p.m. there is a short prayer and then we walk home to sleep.

When Uncle Putu is home from the Anglican Seminary in Johannesburg, he accompanies us to our door. We all love Uncle Putu because he can sing anything, even jazz – and, like his sister Tinnie, he knows all the latest dances, even though he is studying to be a priest. Watching them toss the drink down their throats is rather entertaining. They squinch their faces and shake their heads as if they are swallowing medicine, and each watches the other, taking pleasure in the moment when the liquor hits the right spot in the throat. It is a good example from which we rehearse for our playing house.

Although 'European' liquor is illegal for Africans to drink, every household in my family has a nip of brandy for special visitors. Visitors are so rare that Ouma sometimes forgets where she has hidden the nip.

The kettle on the stove is always ready to be boiled so that I can appear with the tea tray before I am asked. Poking revives the fire. The ashes fall, reviving the coal to a lively fire that soon has the kettle singing and the steam rising in the milk pan. The fire only dies as we sleep during the night. By the age of nine, I have learnt how to wake up at six to remove the ashes and start a fire for the new day without waking the household. First I set the rolled newspapers on the bed, on top of which planks from tomato boxes are crossed to allow the air to circulate and, on top of these, the chopped firewood. The newspaper is lit with Lion matches and as the flames catch, the coals slowly settle on the flames. With a clean chimney the smoke is sucked out and slowly the black shining coals crackle and burst with sparks, drool and hum, then turn to molten red.

THERE IS always something to be done. There is wood to be chopped, the coal bucket to be refilled, water to be collected at the street tap on the corner, under the wattle tree. On Saturdays we wash the windows, do the laundry, weed the flower garden along the side wall of the house leading to the gate, polish the linoleum floors with white Sunbeam polish and the concrete veranda and steps with red polish, and then shine them with a brush and soft cloth from discarded old cotton clothes. These cloths have to be washed and hung out to dry separately because of the strict injunction not to make clean with dirty tools.

One day to my surprise Ouma agrees that I should work in the backyard with the dung, a creative outlet in the daily chores. We gather the still-steaming cow dung in the veld above the township, where the cows graze to the rhythmic sound of the goods train clanging empty carriages to the Witbank Colliery and full carriages returning, piled high with newly mined coal. We mix it into a thick paste with water. On all fours, I do as my ouma has taught me, scooping a handful and spreading it evenly with an open hand to cover the handbroom-swept clay ground. Then, racing against the hot sun, my hand now partly cupped, fingers and thumb slightly spread, I work the dung to create triangles within triangles in a straight line. The pattern is completed with alternating swirls of half-circles below the triangles. Only the buzzing flies from the chicken coop make their last stand and I am lost in the race to cover the whole backyard. When the sun has dried the dung, I sweep the court-yard gently to remove the excess and refine the set pattern. I bask in the rare praise from Ouma, who declares that I am becoming a *regte vroumens* (a real woman). My artistry becomes a favourite topic in the KwaGuqa family. When we wake the morning after my cow-dung painting, my efforts have been washed away by the rain. It so happens that my mother comes on one of her surprise visits and Ouma proudly tells her of my hard work destroyed by the storm. She is not impressed and I hear her saying, 'Her father would not like that. She must spend her time learning how to read and write even better, not wasting it on meaningless work.' When she is gone Ouma tells me she is hurt by Mama's remark. I am graduated to learning how to cook, bake, embroider and knit, and my mother teaches me how to read recipes and knitting patterns in her *Woman's Weekly* magazines, things I hate with all my heart. Every issue has something about the Royal Family and I envy the young prince and his sisters because in the pictures all they seem to do is wear new clothes and smile with the full attention of their happy parents and waving spectators.

After school, tea is with bread, butter and jam. I go to George Mashiyane's grocery store to buy the ingredients for the prepa-ration of the following day's brew. To repeat again the sing-song of one shilling brown sugar, one and sixpence mielie meal, one tickey yeast, two and six *mabele* (sorghum meal). Brown packets folded down, I run back home to help Ouma mix the brew, handing each ingredient to her as she mixes and stirs with the fat wooden spoon. I go on surveillance to the open veld below the railway line for the burying of the new brew and the retrieval of the fermented beer.

Ouma is stern and her rare spontaneity soon turns to anger if my eager questions are too candid. We are not friends. I am her charge and one of the first things I learn is that there can be no parity between us. I am only a child and have to curb my impetuousness, my desire 'to know everything about the business of adults'. *Grootmense* (adults) have their own world; they ration information in bits, and children are expected to know their place. Sometimes, though, an episode from her childhood springs unexpectedly from Ouma's mouth and runs away so she can't catch it. Out of the blue she frequently repeats the account of how, when she was a mere child working in the kitchen of the farm owner, ragged white children tanned by the sun and the dust came to beg for a bit of sugar and salt and milk and a cup of mealie meal to make soft porridge for the baby. As much as I learn to understand that the moral of the story is that I am lucky to have a roof over my head and several meals a day, I also ask the same questions.

Where was their mother and the baby, Ouma?

She was holding the crying baby in the wagon, too proud to come out and ask herself.

And what did you do?

We had been instructed to give them whatever food was available in the kitchen.

And where was the Missus?

Looking through the curtains from the front room and shouting angrily at us all day afterwards.

Why?

You are too young to understand.

Why?

Now go and make me some tea with warm milk and stop asking questions.

She never says why, but my imagination runs wild with images that do not quite fit into the picture that is now firmly fixed in my mind.

In rare moments, I get fuller glimpses into Ouma's life before KwaGuqa. Ouma remembers the South African War. She refers to it as the *groot oorlog* – the big war. She was a child only this high, she shows me with her five fingers clumped together, her wrist bent towards her bosom. She and her sister watched in terror, hiding in the bush as white men on horses hacked off steaks from live, grazing cattle with their swords and braaied them on an open fire. Other times she hid behind the bushes, watching white men stop their covered wagons near the stream running by the farm where she worked in the kitchen. She saw them with their dirt-streaked clothes, helping their barefoot women and children out of the wagons. They came in small waves, rummaging around the fields, then braaiing small birds and chickens to eat. Catching herself in a moment of candour, she pulls back into the present. She admonishes herself: 'That's enough, I must go back to work. *Jy het te veel vragies. Lewe is werk, nie grappies, en Johanna moet gaan werk.*' (You have too many questions. Life is work, not tales, and Johanna must get back to work.) She is removed from herself and often refers to herself as if she were not there.

Much later I begin to understand. Apartheid is designed to permanently erase the memory of that time when whites were dirty, poor, homeless, workless underdogs. It is designed to ensure that a black child will never again see a poor white person. Indeed the new laws under the regime of apartheid are legislated one by one so that no white person should ever be without food, a house, a job, medical care, or an education. Even then I shield myself from imagining my grandmother's life as a child. Instead, I laugh with my peers at their songs, their food, their clothes, their rules, their beliefs, rushing only to adopt the latest of everything.

In her restraint, Ouma never tells me about the wars of attrition in which the Ndebele Ndzundza chiefdom, from which her family came, slowly lost their land, autonomy, ways of life and material freedom. She says nothing about the Voortrekkers who first paid tribute to the early king Mabhogo to be granted the right to use communal land for grazing and cultivating and who, with the active mediation of the early missionaries, soon turned their requests into demands. She does not say that her great-grandfather may have been one of the warriors under the great Chief Nyabela, who succeeded Mabhogo's two sons, who refused at first to surrender to the Pedi King Mampuru, the assassin of the invincible Sekhukhune. She speaks only of the greatness of Chief Mabhogo who died in 1865, he who built a formidable kingdom with a complex of underground tunnels between the fortified caves that were the stronghold of the Ndzundza warriors.

By the time she was born, the Ndebele kingdom was no more. Her people had been vanquished, their land taken by brutal force. It all came to pass under King Nyabela and his regiments, who were starved and then smoked out the caves to be chained, whipped in public and paraded as slaves in public trials, far away in Pretoria. While Mampuru was hanged, Nyabela's sentence of death was commuted to life imprisonment and for fifteen years he languished in jail. The Ndebele land was awarded to the Boers who had fought against Nyabela in the commandos led by General Piet Joubert. The chiefs who paid tribute to Nyabela were scattered, their subjects indentured like slaves to labour on the farms of poor Boers.

As I calculate it now, she was born four years after Chief Nyabela was arrested and she was only about fifteen years old when he died in 1902. To say Nyabela's name aloud must have been a crime, just as it was with Mandela in the decades before his release. Nyabela's fate was well known, but not his face.

What she knows about amaNdebele she has patched together from hearsay, rumour, eavesdropping and furtive recollections from traumatised narrators speaking in secret, or from the epithets of white bigots with snaking sjamboks. Or the parables of missionary sermons reaching out pacify and to warn about what lay ahead for the ones who disobeyed *baasskap* (white authority). She learnt all about herself and her people in the farm kitchens where she had worked since she was waist-high. She could not have known joy or pleasure but she is familiar with physical fatigue, with endurance and with an anger she does not dare to name.

She does not say that they were the surviving remnants of a polity in which everyone in the vicinity had played a role in the competition to strip them of their material and psychological worth – and that, when they became tenants on their own land, they still had to scatter all over the country, working at anything to earn the money they were expected to pay for taxes as tenants on the very land where their umbilical cords were buried. The ignominy piled on the king, Nyabela – humiliated, deposed and then imprisoned – was the hallmark of her adolescence. For many of the Africans living in the area between Middelburg and Pretoria the missionary stations were a haven. It is estimated that around the area of Botshabelo in Middleburg there were more than thirty Lutheran mission stations.

The name from her past that Ouma repeats with consistency

is that of Reverend Ernst Ludwig Gustav Eiselen, a Prussian missionary who translated the Bible and Lutheran Hymnal into Sepedi and spoke fluent isiNdebele. He was based at the Berlin Mission Society in Botshabelo (Place of Refuge). His figure looms large in her memories. One particular sermon he delivered at the mission station where she worshipped when she was a young woman working on the farm was fixed in her brain. It would not let her go and, unwittingly, she imprinted it on our yet-innocent minds. When she was about fifteen years old, in the years immediately after the end of the South African War in 1902, Johanna prepared for her confirmation into the Berlin Lutheran Church. She knew how to read the Dutch Bible and had committed the catechism to memory. At the mission station they had also been taught how to cook, sew, bake and carry out the related domestic services required to work in a European household.

They had been told that a senior pastor would conduct the service. He would preach to them in Sepedi, which he spoke perfectly. First he congratulated the confirmands on their rejection of heathenism and warned them sternly against backsliding. Then he turned to congratulate them on their fine European clothing. He noted that their clothes were impeccable and surpassed the humble style of the missionaries, who had sacrificed everything to come and teach them the Word of the Lord. 'You must not aim to equal those whom God has sent to uplift you from the depths of heathenism,' he said. 'You will never be their equals, for as the Bible says you are the children of Ham. Your role in His kingdom is to be the hewers of wood and the drawers of water. You must always remember that. You can never be like Europeans. They have been chosen by God to uplift you and you have been saved so that you can help them to fulfil that role. Your fancy clothes and mimicking of

European mannerisms is going to come to an end. You will once more be placed where you belong. Now gather yourselves up and serve the Lord in the truth of His Holy Word, just as He has ordained. All of this frippery is going to come to an end in your very lifetime.'

Although he was known for his severity and aloofness, it was a seminal experience for Ouma and, perhaps unknown to her then, Eiselen's message of doom was seeded in her being. His son would go on to be Secretary of Native Affairs between 1949 and 1960, and Chief Inspector of Native Education in the Transvaal between 1936 and 1946.

Ouma fears whites, and it is a source of great questioning in my mind when I consider her marriage to Walter Bower. I still wonder now. Was he white or had he decided to leave Ladysmith to pass for white? What was their courtship like? Did he not decide to pass for white far away from Ladysmith, where he could play the role of Scots gentleman? Does it really matter if there was never a romance between them? Is the fact that they had two children four years apart proof of a love liaison? However she experienced and understood her relationship with Walter, Ouma's hanging of their framed marriage certificate on the front room wall presented a constant reminder to her and to everyone who entered her home of their relationship and its formalisation before the church and state.

✤ ✤ ✤

OUR PARENTS are visitors who come in time for Christmas, Easter, or an odd weekend, unless there is a funeral. But on Christmas Day even the meanest join in the cry of, 'Heppie, heppie. Where is the Christmas Box?' An uncalled truce reigns, filling the place with temporary merriment and noise that takes the older folk back to remember times that we know only from hearsay, times when they were young and lived on the farms in Middelburg, near Doornkop, or Groblersdal, dressed in their best to go to the Sunday service at the mission station.

On Fridays and Saturdays, the town bristles with farmers from the surrounding rural areas bringing their produce to the market and themselves lording it and monopolising the water-hosed streets. One day, when Minkie is still living in Witbank with us and I am about five years old, our visiting mother takes Minkie and me to buy shoes in town. My brother is dressed in a navy-blue and white sailor suit and I am wearing a smocked pink dress with red roses embroidered on the bodice, all brought from the big city for us. The three of us walk past as some white children alight from the back of a blue bakkie streaked with dry red mud, while their hefty parents heave their way out of the front seats.

It happens very quickly. In an instant our day out with Mama is spoiled; something we will remember all our lives happens. The strident voice of a boy child sitting in the open back of the bakkie shouts, '*Ma, kyk, die bobbejaanties het nuwe klere aan!*' (Ma, look, the little monkeys are wearing new clothes!)

My heart is beating so hard from fear: I hear Mama asking the child's mother in Afrikaans, 'Does your child fill you with pride?' Then something unexpected happens. The white man getting out of the driver's seat takes the boy who uttered the *bobbejaan* word by the scruff of the neck and slaps him once in the face with his open hand. '*Hoeveel keer moet ek vir jou dieselfde ding sê?*' (How many times must I tell you the same thing?)

My mother is holding our hands tight, squeezing so hard that it hurts. 'My babies, don't mind him. He has not been taught couth.'

The white man rushes towards us. He stops in front of us,

and when he raises his big hand towards his brow I think he is going to strike my mother. On either side the space between his knee-length grey socks and his short khaki pants is the size of a big tree trunk, bigger than my petite mother's waistline. Towering over us, he stops and quickly leans forward as though he is about to bow. '*Verskoon ons, Mevrou.*' (Excuse us, Madam). He promptly turns and marches back to his bakkie's driver's seat. We walk away, a hand each in my mother's two small hands, firm in her trembling grasp.

❖ ❖ ❖

THERE ARE some grannies who receive money each month-end from their children who work on the Reef. Some of them supplement their allowance by doing laundry at their homes, for white families. The older children under their care collect the dirty laundry in bundles and then deliver it and collect the payment. In the location, the owners of the laundry are discussed casually regarding the condition and amount of the soiled laundry they produce, and how at times they nonchalantly postpone payment. The merits of doing laundry for the English or the Afrikaners are enthusiastically discussed, as is the state of their households as viewed from outside the kitchen – if they got in that far. It is not unusual for the delivery person to wait at the gate, in rain or shine or bitter cold, until a worker opens it to collect the laundry or let them in. At any rate, it is preferable not to risk sniffing dogs let loose on purpose for the amusement of the children or the missus peeking through the lace curtains. Some of the madams are kind and receive the bundles directly, giving water or leftover food and old clothes, even asking after the health of the washerwoman.

When my mother is studying for her social work diploma,

Johanna takes in washing, but by the time I go to school she no longer works for whites and we manage by selling beer and with my mother's monthly allowance sent through the post office. As self-employed women, my granny and her ilk consider themselves respectable businesswomen and they make a significant contribution to the church collection on Sundays. I do not remember that there was a stigma attached to selling liquor and I never felt uncomfortable around other children coming from working homes. It is only when my father's relatives visit that there is some unease on Ouma's part. Then my routine is changed to sit and eat in the front room with them.

Everyone who comes to visit from the big towns presses a gift of money into Ouma's hand when they depart. But none are as generous as my Uncle Kenny, who outdoes even my parents. Because Ouma does not have a *toggie* (piece job), I have no interaction with white people, except for policemen. This is true of most of my peers. In our childhood we are cocooned away from direct contact with white people, most of the time. My grandmother loves the British Royal Family and keeps cuttings of their doings in the drawer of the front-room sideboard. I happen to be on holiday in Payneville with my parents when the Royal Family visits South Africa in 1948. At the time my mother is already working at the crèche and community welfare centre in Payneville as a social worker. Her supervisor is a white woman whose husband is the supervisor of the municipality. She calls the black women at the crèche *my meisie* (my girl). We practise songs and wear our best clothes for the fleeting royal visit to the township. Like children in most South African towns, we wait for what seems to be half the day in the scorching sun for a glimpse of the Royal Family. When it arrives, the Royal Motorcade zips past us so quickly that we don't even have time to wave our miniature Union Jacks.

✧ ✧ ✧

IN LATER years Ouma claims to come from the Ndzundza chiefdom of the Ndebele people. But then she also calls herself a Manala. IsiNdebele – a Nguni language, like isiZulu – has many Sepedi and Afrikaans words in it. Like the Swazi and the Tswana, the legendary armies of Mzilikazi, who had fled Zululand and finally established another kingdom of his own in Bulawayo, in present-day Zimbabwe, are the stuff of storytelling. The destruction of the Sekhukhune and Ndzundza entities by the settlers was not a once-off event, but long and drawn out with episodes of an uneasy trust on the part of the Ndebele broken by the unremitting land greed of the Voortrekkers. With the help of the early missionaries and the authorities of the ZAR (the Zuid-Afrikaansche Republiek or South African Republic, which later became the Transvaal province), the Voortrekkers forcibly appropriated the best land. Ouma and her generation were the immediate descendants of recently vanquished men and women. Their surviving elders had fresh memories still covered up in the piety of new Christian converts. They could only survive by forgetting what they remembered. They remained stripped of land, they were stripped of chiefs, and they were separated from one another and distributed among the Dutch farmers like chattels. Some stayed near where they had owned land but by Ouma's womanhood many had fled to the new towns near the mines. A common saying in the African community was that the whites came bearing the gift of the Bible and in exchange they took the land and kept the guns to themselves.

Despite their heroic efforts in diplomacy and hard-fought wars against the settlers, the Ndebele and Pedi chiefdoms were ultimately defeated. But it was the Ndebeles whose land was plundered, whose livestock was looted, whose women and children were indentured and who subsequently lived a life of servitude, with entire communities ripped apart and scattered. The ravenous hunger for their land and labour, the relentless demand for taxes and tributes, and their own role as surrogates in earlier long, drawn-out skirmishes initiated for the self-interest of the British and the Boers brought them to their knees.

At the centre of the mayhem was the established presence of the strong Berlin Mission Society. It may have been a place of refuge for new converts and the displaced, but it was also a mini state that exacted tithes and fines, and the obedience of the children of those who lived within it. Through its own economic success, it surpassed the ZAR, which was virtually insolvent and could not provide succour to the greedy demands of the Boer farmers. The German missionaries, ethnologists and zealots of *volkskunde* (cultural anthropology) represented a religious imperialism grounded in the Prussian intellectual ideology of respect and fealty to the rulers, which simultaneously gave them the latitude to interpret, translate and be the go-betweens for the powers that be and their conquered subjects. While they were defending their faith and developing their property – using the labour of the converts – their loyalty lay with the ruling government.

At first dislocated and dispossessed by the Trekker Boers, the newly landless were further impoverished by the ensuing Anglo-Boer Wars, which trapped them in a continuous cycle of uncertainty and instability. Reduced to tenants on the very land that had once belonged to them, irregularly paid by the exploitative Boer farmers and faced with summary evictions when payday arrived, the allure of the diamond, gold and coal mines sucked them into the logical position of pioneer African urban dwellers. In this mix were the early *inboekelinge*, indentured servants who were virtual slaves and whose debt was renewed whenever it was time for them to be freed. They were

Griquas and Khoi and San who had come as slaves and *agterryers*, highly skilled artisans who had in some cases been drafted into the exodus to the north by the early Trekkers.

In virtual terms, many African children and women also laboured under the same conditions, especially when they were captured in the early confrontations with the early settlers. Some historical records show that special brigades were organised to capture children to work on the white farms. In fact, the Trekkers who left the Cape in the early nineteenth century did so in defiance of, and deep bitterness about, the abolition of slavery. They felt unfairly deprived of what they considered their most valuable possession: their slaves, without whose unpaid labour they could not survive. Not least among the reasons for their exodus from the Cape Colony was their racially inspired hatred of the status of the indigenous Khoi and San, whose offspring from mixed liaisons with Europeans had created a deep revulsion grounded in the Boers' Calvinistic religious beliefs. Besides, they had been isolated from mainstream Cape society and, with their rusticity and poor educational background, abhorred the material trappings of the Colony. They were trapped in the past, unable to come to terms with change.

The scarcity of everyday information about the lives of early black urban dwellers in the first urban locations is numbing. Unless you are an academic focused on research, it is almost impossible to get a quick representation of African social history. It is only in the fictional works of the earlier writers such as Es'kia Mphahlele, Alex La Guma and Peter Abrahams, for example, that one gets some view of black life. Even then, there is, understandably, minor focus on the actual history that got them there, except from the point of view of the great hunger for their labour. Of course what seem to matter most are detailed analyses of the rush for minerals, and Africans are mere statistical units.

They are not full-blown humans but mere 'also theres', depicted as footnotes in the grand history of South Africa's industrial development. They are highlighted only in terms of 'disturbances', political hindrances and exceptions. Were it not for the 'new' historians like Sol Plaatje, Peter Delius, Bernard Mbenga, Bongani Ngqulunga, Jack Simons and many others, who probe events from the point of view of Africans, we would know even less about the actual role of these formidable pioneers of modern urban life. Unfortunately, trawling through the archives of libraries, newspapers and foundations is the stuff of a few scholars and hardly the civic undertaking of the general population, the majority of whom simply do not have libraries in their townships, the luxury of time, or the patience and education. For the ordinary man, woman or child needing quick reference about themselves and the past, it is a matter of hearsay and popular magazines, or electronic devices that only supply the latest untested postings. Sadly, the only references to KwaGuqa are mostly about coal. It is in this fashion that I discovered that Witbank was also famed by association with Winston Churchill. In my time it was not even known that he had ever set foot near Witbank.

Churchill was a war correspondent for a British newspaper, *The Morning Post*, during the Anglo-Boer War when he was captured and imprisoned in Pretoria. He escaped imprisonment to make his way east to Witbank, on his way to the Portuguese colony of Mozambique. There, he was helped by a friendly British mine manager who hid him under the coal bags on a coal train on its way from the Witbank Colliery to Delagoa Bay. That story, of a white man hiding under dirty coal bags, is never told to us in the history lessons. But we all know of Jan van Riebeeck and the three ships that landed on the virgin shores of the southernmost Cape, an untouched land waiting to be cultivated and to be penetrated and bled till it yielded its fruit. *Reiger, Drommedaris,*

De Goede Hoop, the ships' names are engraved in my memory. We have to know the names of the European characters, the dates, their ships, by heart for the examinations. Scraps of information still stick in my craw today – how they suffered from a disease called scurvy, how they needed fresh vegetables, and on and on. But little was said about how, nine months after their arrival, there was born a new group of South Africans who would forever bear the burden of definition and acceptance. It would be the mothers of these children who would bear the scrutiny of blame and judgement. Without power or any authority, they were deemed responsible for the existence of this new South African tribe. But of the stench that accompanied the landing of the ships and how it had spread over the land for centuries and engulfed all in a snarl, on that the history books are silent. Pacification, cattle thieves, laziness, love of liquor, appeasement … these words I remember and parrot. But in every school, in every location, there is that teacher who dares to teach differently.

These costumes of the discoverers were not echoed in the clothing of the working men we called Boetie, Oompie, Oupa or Baba. Yes, we were taught that older people could only be addressed by the names we called their peers in our own families, with a prefix to their names. Chafed and under the unremitting humiliation of a conquered people, African children were invested in an exclusive culture of respect for the old. We were enveloped within a fragile sanctuary of community interdependence and our emergence was usually forced by a traumatic incident of violence perpetrated by a white person on someone in the family or community. Few of us knew that, all over the world, in Asia, Latin America, the Caribbean and the rest of Africa, there were also people who had to lead a double life, putting on a face for the workplace where they were called upon to answer to the names of John, Jim and Mary, or Kaffir and Apie, or whatever was spat out by the baas or the missus or the *kleinbasie* (young boss).

In the morning, the men and women, whom we call Auntie, Gogo, Baba, Uncle, Sisi, go to the workplace. When the clock strikes or the siren sounds at the end of the workday (*tshayile* time), they take off the aprons and the overalls, and their invisible masks. They retrieve some part of themselves and take pleasure in being able to forget the workplace until the sun rises again. They may be accosted on the way home by police seeking their passes or proof that they have paid one tax or another. Many others gain their temporary relaxation by passing on enamelled mugs of home brew, drunk in establishments such as the one that Ouma runs. It is their equivalent of going to the bar or the country club. For a few hours they enjoy the illusion of home, having drinks, telling jokes, sharing stories and revelling in the camaraderie in the houses of these old women with strict regulations who dispense advice, ask after their kin and send them home when they have had enough to drink. I do not recall that anybody was ever robbed or seduced in our house. We had no stabbings or fights of any sort. It was just a pleasant hum of conversation and a sharing of fellowship.

IN KWAGUQA we also boast a few veterans from World War II. While they were not allowed to carry arms when they enlisted in South Africa, the exigencies of the war situation at the front forced their South African commanders to ignore the racial imperatives of their country and arm them to defend democracy. Verified accounts of battles demonstrate that, in Egypt, Ethiopia and German South West Africa, South African blacks showed their mettle in major battles and made a solid contribution to the success of the Allied Forces against the Germans.

Again, at my Anglican school in KwaGuqa there is that young male teacher who sets aside the textbook from time to time. That teacher tells us that kneeling down is not an isolated part of our past. He says it has not always been the case that we have been without power. He says that every one of us has something inside us that nobody can touch. It is the knowledge of ourselves, the knowledge that is not in the schoolbooks. He says we come from warriors and sages and that in our veins is the blood of those warriors, of whom we must remain proud despite the lies we have been told about them. He says that, every day when we come to school, we must call on the name of one king of the many who said no. He says that nothing remains the same forever and that we need to know that we can bring change.

Ouma says that her coming to Witbank meant that Reverend Eiselen had been right in his prediction that they would be brought to their knees, where they belonged. Eiselen was a disciple of Alexander Merensky of the Berlin Mission Society. When Merensky's attempts to set up a mission station in their territories were firmly rejected by King Sobhuza of the Swazis and King Sekhukhune of the Pedis in the early 1860s, he moved to Middelburg where he founded Botshabelo, which became the leading station of the Berlin Society in South Africa. This area, the theatre of the first incursions by those early Dutch Voortrekkers still bitter with the English for depriving them of their slaves in the Cape, and hungry for land, was also not far from Pilgrim's Rest – where, in 1874, gold was discovered. Subsequently, Barberton in the 1880s gold rush also became a magnet for adventurers, speculators, prospectors, hunters, shopkeepers, smugglers in search of quick riches, with successive ZAR and British colonial administrators in tow to exact their own pound of flesh.

By 1889 the area between Witbank and Middelburg had four

coal mines, which supplied fuel to the gold mines in Johannesburg. Able-bodied men, the memory of conquest still fresh in their minds, had no choice but to work on the mines. Their world of land farming and stock farming had been replaced with a rapacious farm system which now required them to be share-croppers on the very lands they had formerly owned, pummelled and subdued by long wars of attrition, in some of which they had fought on the side of the Dutch ZAR and in others the English colonists. Peace, when it was visiting, was short-lived, and it exacted heavy payment from the Ndebele and the Pedi: it was the newly defeated Boers who were rewarded with land, live-stock and the forced labour of the very men who had faced them down in battle at a time when a black man could own a gun. The Boers, the British, the Ndebele, the Swazis and the Pedis did not share a common motive for entering into these battles. While the former two groups fought for domination and the greater power of the ZAR and the British colony respectively, the Africans were fighting for their very survival as strong agricultural entities with a right to raise their families in the lands they had cultivated, near the rivers and in the mountains – which were also their last-ditch hiding places.

Out of the upheavals of the Mfecane earlier in the previous century, from which they had wrought their small nation-states, strong men and women contested the right to inhabit the spaces that grew smaller as hordes of Boers claimed greater space to grow and to settle. Griqua and Khoisan, Bakone and Ndebele, Pedi and Swazi – some in the pay of European adventurers and traders – were wending their way to the Kimberley diamond mines. It was preferable to the black men to work in the mines on contract so that they could buy guns and own cattle, rather than to toil on the ill-equipped farms owned by the Boers, who often forced their labour and paid them a pittance. It may be that some wanted to buy back their children and womenfolk, who were indentured to these farmers in an informal system of slavery that was based on race. Mixed into this poison were the missionaries who, by and large, chose to follow the law of the ZAR. In the long run, it was they who became the instruments ensuring that the different taxes were collected to shore up the Boer republic.

They are all dead and gone now, but in stubborn remembrance my family hovers in my mind and lingers as part of who I am now. They cannot reproach me for my inaccuracies, nor can they deny me the licence to recapture the nourishment of their imperfect lives on my own. I may have been a quiet child, as they said I was, but I think I was always an outward-looking one too. As a child I have a notion that the KwaGuqa skies are like an enclosing canopy that lock me in, away from my mother and my father and all the attention that is showered on my elder brother Minkie, later popularly known as Hugh, his school name. Unlike the stolid grandmothers who raised me in Witbank Location I am always searching for the end of the horizon, intrigued by what lies beyond it, unwilling to succumb to the shackles of childhood obedience. My brother, two years older than me, leaves me to live with our parents in City Deep, Johannesburg, where our father works as a mine clerk. He was my first friend. Now, I cannot recall my emotions when he left, but then, he spends all the school holidays with us in KwaGuqa and I revel in his presence, as I did always, afterwards. His return to my parents renders me tearful and sulking. I am a downcast little girl, wallowing in the anguish that separates me from my parents. From the first I have been enjoined to set aside my yearnings and submit myself to the will of my elders, and smile like a good girl. But at times I cannot rearrange my facial muscles to hide the war in my heart.

In time I learn not to display my displeasure and to modulate my responses with an unquestioning acknowledgement of the authority that comes with age. It is an act I have to learn, in order to get by. Like girl children everywhere in that age, I am raised to understand that what awaits me is pain, sorrow, hardship and loss, because men travel and at times they do not return, cannot return. But they always die and leave you behind. Endurance is to be my aspiration: women were created to give birth and raise children, often with the possibility of outliving them.

My best friends are my cousins Wincie, Miriam and, later, Dineo. They live with Ouma Martha, Ouma's sister – Ouma Sussie. We are closely knit and their house is like a second home to me. We crowd around my great-grandmother, Gogo, who reigns quietly, sitting in the shade of the fig tree, busy making and selling snuff. Her daughters take turns with her ablutions and meals and her daily journey from her room to her shaded post under the fig tree. Her voluminous black robes often serve as a refuge when we are threatened with hidings by our sister grannies. They do not dare touch us in her presence. Her croaky voice, rarely heard, is the last word. She dies suddenly and without fuss when I am eight years old. Hardly six months later, Oupa Jacobus follows after a struggle with a chest infection, probably silicosis. My grannies are still cloaked in black when my uncle, Uncle Bower, dies two months later.

From the beginning, when I become aware of my plight, I think of Ouma as an obstacle. She stands between my parents and me. I cannot live with them because I am a girl. It is not easy to raise a girl child in the city, the old people say with finality. There is no argument, then, to trump what to them is a time-worn truth. Besides, all my playmates in the family are also living apart from their parents. My femalehood floats in the air like the dry leaves in the seasonal winds that buffet our lives unchangingly. And neither the frequent rain of tears nor the gasps of broken breath that seize my scraggly body can change my fate. I am a girl, my mother is in training at the Jan H Hofmeyr School of Social Work and I need an old woman's hand to shape me into a woman. I am to remain with Ouma until I am twelve years old, when we move to live with my parents, together. She sells her stand at number 76 Tollman Street, most of her belongings and all of her chickens. We count the money in our bedroom at night when everybody has left, as we have been doing every night since I was seven years old. She has accumulated over five hundred pounds and she swears me to silence never to reveal her worth to anyone, especially Thomas, my father, who has never paid lobola and who has not paid for his own wife's training at the Jan Hofmeyr School. The money will be saved, she said, until a piece of land can be found to build herself a small house of her own.

Yes, my ouma is an orphan woman, fending for herself, alone in the world, without a husband. The only one she has left is Pannie, my mother. Over the years we have grown close in our own way and I have begun to understand that men die and women fall, then get up. They get up to mourn and then take care of business.

MY GRANNY sisters were raised under the rigorous influence of the Berlin Lutheran missionaries, strict segregationists who believed strongly in separating religious and ethnic identity. I know nothing of the praise names or songs of the Ndebele people because there was never anyone to recite them to me. At high school in the heart of Zululand, my schoolmates recite reams of poetry praising their forebears. They even know the praise songs of other Zulu clans not related to them, by heart. My Ndebele forebears are unsung. They have been silenced by the swords, the guns and the Bible of the settlers and the missionaries.

But the name of Mabhogo remains in the air, as does the exclamation 'Mabogoli!' It is only Gogo's grey eyes and light skin that hint at something forever unspoken. Wisps of grey, silky, straight hair break free from her black Dutch *kappie* (bonnet), and are always firmly stuffed back underneath it.

In our world, touching or saying I love you is not done. Only babies enjoy that indulgence, not long-limbed boys and girls, dreaming of escape. Our only link to the past is the Mabena name. Our elders were tough. It is as if they stuffed the tribulations of their past in a bag, sprinkled it with white wax, set it to kindle and walked away. The wind never comes but the embers twinkle still. It is the expediency of having arrived in KwaGuqa, rather than why or how they got there, that matters.

The march of work is Ouma's balm, as is her endless humming of nameless songs. It is decades later that I begin to understand why anger, longing, resentment and death were the forces that drove us closer together. She put the lid on my curiosity and shut me into an incompleteness, a bane that over time was changed into a great motivator. As I look back now, that need to know spurred me on. She enabled me to break through to the possibilities that were forbidden to women of her time. She had, in a big way, done things that that many of her peers had never dreamt of – gone to faraway places like the Kimberley diamond diggings to seek her own fortune – and I glory in the secrets she kept from me and that I had to seek out for myself. I take pride in the women of her league, the ones who made their way to the chaotic cities of their time to become the first urban dwellers in Johannesburg, Barberton, Lydenburg: all the towns that sprouted around the mines. These brave women are given short shrift in colonial history books. They are referred to as loose women, prostitutes, kept women and the like. Now, I see them as pioneers, unaided by present-day popular norms to fit into a prescribed mould of heroism. The education they acquired was strictly for menial and religious purposes only. In the grand plan of white superiority, there were no institutions designed with the notion of raising them higher than child-bearers and farm labourers. In fact, they were the ones who first challenged the traditional strictures of gender: even in the limited space of their precarious daily survival, they had to meet the contingencies thrust upon them by both traditional custom and colonial rule. Their feminism grew out of necessity; they did not have the luxury of discussing it in symposia and workshops.

Indeed, we must respect them not so much for challenging the norms of patriarchy as for their perspicacity in grappling with the practical realities thrust upon them. The overarching value shared by all South African men, irrespective of race or origin, at all times of South African history, is the perpetuation of the dominant role of men over women. It was unquestionable! The unspeakable manifestation of gender-based violence today is a logical outcome of a historical patriarchy that has evolved over generations in style and intensity but has always reflected the shape of our society as a whole.

For the most part, their men were dead, indentured, enslaved, imprisoned, turned into migrants or simply rendered impotent to play the customary role of protecting and sheltering women. Under the circumstances, the women stepped into the breach and became the heads of households. True, they maintained a deference to the social imperatives dictated by tradition and cus-tom, but by doing this they neutralised the patriarchal forces in their own culture and set themselves free to pursue their goals of self-reliance without inviting the hostility of an already decimated self-worth in their male counterparts who had already been emasculated by conquest and almost totally humiliated. They still bowed down to the prescripts of male authority. No family council was complete without a male elder, even when he was only a neighbour. His presence and his counsel legitimised decisions affecting serious family matters, but in fact it was the women who formulated the problem that was to be solved and identified the necessity of male participation in the decision-making, to legitimise the recommended action.

Kneeling, stooping and bending are postures required by much of women's work. Scrubbing floors on all fours, polishing concrete floors, polishing them with a hand-held brush, portion by portion, then rubbing them with a cloth till they shine, washing soiled nappies, snotty handkerchiefs, men's and women's under- and outerwear on a washboard in a zinc bath, spreading cow dung, baking, dusting furniture, sweeping floors with hand-held grass brooms, wiping backsides of children with old newspapers, cooking on a Welcome Dover stove or on an open fire outside the house and more – women knelt and stooped.

Wa tsho u Eiselen (Eiselen declared) is my ouma's favourite mantra. It is her response to the creeping reach of violence and racism that tears into the fabric of personal lives and rips apart every semblance of dignity and respect for the claim of a single humanity. As we grow wiser and older, Minkie and I raise our eyebrows, nodding knowingly at her as she arranges her sombre face to spit out, once again, Eiselen's name. In later years, oceans away, *Wa tsho* becomes a watchword to remind us of what we are and to remember where we come from. Eiselen had indeed told them – in a sermon, *nogal* (for that matter) – that Africans would be brought to their knees where they belonged. They had barely entered their adulthood, expecting something better than the evictions and scatterings that would become the lasting motif of their improbable lives.

It was not as though the British edict against slavery would ever have made the indigenes their equals. It was the resentment of former conquerors, the Dutch, rejecting the dominion of their own vanquishers – the British, Europeans like themselves, urbane and suave, in contrast to the Dutch, with their inbred rusticity and plodding subservience to the past. The feeling of an imposed inequality is not always overt. It is in the gesture, in words that are unsaid, in the manner in which an unwitting pedestrian occurrence diminishes you unexpectedly. This is what the Dutch felt in the presence of the vaunting English conquerors.

In *Wild Conquest* by Peter Abrahams, a young Dutch girl, Elsie, is on a rare trip to Cape Town with her rural family and sees an English lady in her carriage.

'The lady's head is high. All the heads of English ladies were high. All the clothes English ladies wore were beautiful. The man beside the lady in the carriage has his head bent and the lady is smiling with her head high.'

The rustic girl, captive in the moment, stands and stares till the carriage disappears. She is left undone, 'uncompleted'.

Similarly, the early African converts were pressed into what they were told would be salvation, a spiritual Eden – but in reality it was never to be, in their corporeal life. They were coerced into a life of hard work, obedience and denial, but this was always to be overlaid by a consciousness of what had been before the white man came. They may not have had firsthand experience of it, but their vanquished elders recreated for them a vanished world that was contradicted by their actual lives. Propelled by the adoption of a promise of the Beyond, their promise was only to be spectators to their own bondage. While the Boers were obsessed by the imperative to erase their humiliation by the English, ultimately the Africans became the tools that constructed the prosperity of both groups. In addition to everything else that diminished their humanity, the oppressed were also weighed down by the contradictions they had to deny in order to survive.

These were some of the realities of my grandmother's past. Much of it was inscribed not in history books but in her living memory.

What Eiselen said on the day of my ouma's confirmation never let her go, and unwittingly she imprinted it on our young minds. To this day, the name Eiselen conjures an image of my ouma trapped in a moment of dread she could never escape. Whatever the circumstances of her marriage to the supposed Scotsman Walter Bower from faraway Ladysmith, I suspect it was to exorcise that prophecy.

I was too young to understand the meaning of the story, and now, long after the fact, I have tried to put myself in her shoes. I know, now, why I was always so stiff and uneasy in the presence of white people, to the dismay of my mother, who wanted them to know that I was a smart child. It was not so much that I was shy but mainly that I held back from them.

But it was the replaying of Eiselen's words that was to be at the core of her every argument in the conversations that took place as I grew up. She could never shake off that encounter at the church. She feared whites, and this is a source of great questioning in my mind when I consider her marriage to Walter Bower. Was he not, in fact, a product of a liaison between unequals, a child who grew up in the backrooms of the master's main house? Does it really matter that there was never a romance between them? Who cares? Was she just one of those 'loose women'?

Ouma's tenant, Uncle Basie, worked at the Witbank Dry Cleaners and he often brought a copy of the *Witbank News* after work. He told of the stories in the paper about the *swart gevaar* (black peril) and the National Party government that was blatantly declaiming its intentions to put the natives in their place.

Nothing could have indicated more clearly than the declaration of Afrikaans as an official language in addition to English that the intention of DF Malan's government was to turn back the clock. I was only seven years old in 1948, the year after my sister Elaine was born, but I was already reading English and I could sense the looming dangers ahead. The voices of the adults grew louder as the lines of speculation about the future grew in parallel to the revelations about the German concentration camps. There was a certain Dr WWM Eiselen who was now the Secretary of Native Affairs, having previously been the Transvaal's Chief Inspector of Native Education. Yes, he was the son of the same Ernst Ludwig Gustav Eiselen, the one who had forewarned my ouma's catechism graduates not to act out above their ordained station.

In the years during World War II and immediately thereafter, the racial distinctions had blurred temporarily and black men had only poor white women as their rivals in the job market. The government of General Smuts had pledged several battalions to the war effort, thus opening up a temporary new space for jobs in the burgeoning industrial sector.

Prior to this, there had been little appetite for training Africans as skilled labourers. In addition there were growing numbers of successful strikes, and the labour movement under the leadership of Clements Kadalie had made strong inroads among African miners. Witbank had a reputation for some of the most successful strikes in the mining industry. Wages had improved and many African workers were able to send their children for secondary education and teacher and nursing training. The various denominations of missionary schools established all over the country in the nineteenth century played a major role in this regard.

My mother was one of the youthful residents of KwaGuqa who entered the Wesleyan Kilnerton Training Institution to study teaching, the leading and most viable profession for Africans. In general, the status of Africans was changing for the better – to the dismay of Afrikaners, who made up the poor white class of South Africa. With the rise of manufacturing industries, the employment of Africans as semi-skilled labourers increased, as did their wages, which outstripped the growth of those of white workers. The ascent of Africans to higher levels of education, including medicine and other sciences, and the growing influence of Fort Hare University and other higher learning institutions for Africans in the face of the conspicuous poverty of the poor white classes, was a challenge to the white supremacists, who were greater in number than the English-speaking whites. The Afrikaners, the majority of whom were of the poor white class with little education, had stiff competition from the black labour class. Major industry was dominated by English speakers. Afrikaners, carrying grudges from the past, did not have a foothold in the running of the economy. They were threatened by the possibility of being swamped by the growing social and economic progress of the Africans. The possibility of a growing class of black Englishmen was anathema to them, leading to a growing fear of the *swart gevaar*.

It was on this fertile ground of unresolved historical issues that the seed of apartheid was sown. The half-hearted attempts to improve the social and economic status of Africans, stillborn in the 1910 Union of South Africa and buried in the 1913 Land Act, had given rise to a fierce Afrikaner nationalism, which was pitted against an equally ferocious growth of African nationalism led by the militant Youth League of the African National Congress. It is in these tense political conditions that the National Party under the leadership of DF Malan came to win the 1948 elections that changed the course of this country's history.

Once more, the pass laws that had been instituted during the

British colonial era were tightened and subsequent restrictions on every aspect of the lives of Africans were entrenched in law. In KwaGuqa, the rumours were thick about the intention to remove the residents to a new township called Lynnville, named after Superintendent Lynn of the municipality. By then, Witbank had become one of the leading coal producers in the country, spurred on by the expansion of gold mining on the Reef and in tandem with the efficient railway that carried men and goods via Johannesburg and the Reef to Lourenço Marques in Mozambique.

The story, then, of how Africans came to Witbank is blurred. It is only the moving from place to place, away from the Middelburg area and scattering all along the little towns with curious names: Ogies, Minnaar, Schoongezicht, Bronkhorstspruit, Delmas and the like.

And so we called Witbank KwaGuqa, the place of kneeling. As a child I always thought of the kneeling in terms of burying the four-gallon tin of beer in the ground. As I grew older and understood our lives better, the kneeling came to encompass our entire way of life.

✤ ✤ ✤

AN ASIAN family owns the two buses that ferry people from Witbank station via the market past the charge office and municipal office through the main street of the location to the entrance of the coal mine. There are the few youngish men who have never made it to Johannesburg and beyond to the small Reef mines and factories, who work as cleaners, gardeners, painters and builders, and at the coal vendor. We also have a shoemaker, a dressmaker and a tailor, but the ownership of a Singer sewing machine is a mark of progress equal to that of owning a Welcome

Dover coal stove. At the heart of the township are the women, leaning towards their sixties, who are the washerwomen, the cooks and the nannies for the poor white railway workers and petty administrators of Native Affairs.

As children we are pretty much sheltered from the reality of the so-called European world, which lies a few miles from our location. For us, little girls, the most prized toy is a blonde, blue-eyed doll with fat arms and legs and moving joints. Though smooth and fragile-looking, the exterior surface of the doll is brittle and hard to the touch. It lies on blood-red foil, all dressed up in pink. Too soon these papier-mâché wonders will be pock-marked, amputated, bald, one-eyed and battered. Grimy little fingers will gouge and scratch, eagerly seeking the source of the wonderment inside these still figures. Yet the crippled doll can still sob the single word 'Mama!' and when you pour water into its mouth it wets itself. Mine lies pristine in its box on top of the wardrobe and I am only allowed to play with it on special occasions and under strict supervision. It is a precious present and, like everything I have been given, it has to be carefully taken care of for someone else to enjoy when I no longer have use for it. I am put off by its rigidity. Just like the porcelain dinner set, the silver cutlery and the white tablecloths, all neatly stored in the drawers and shelves of the large sideboard set against the wall in the front room, it is like a futile chore. The crockery is only taken out when we have visitors or when Oupa Legoale, the chief interpreter at the Witbank Court, comes for tea. For our every-day use, there is an enamel-plated set of crockery. It is way before the use of plastic, which, as someone would much later remark, would become the national flower of South Africa.

Also in our kitchen, the newly installed coal stove pops and snaps as the flickers turn into flames, splintering the coals and shooting minute crackling missiles. Occasionally a lazy oil-like substance sputters then expires into an orchestra of a thousand small murmuring explosions. We keep the stove door open to make sure that the ensuing smoke travels smoothly into the chimney and out, to announce the end or the beginning of the day. The damper that controls the passage of air is up and will only be lowered to preserve the fire when the black coals are bloody hot and free of smoke. We learn early in life that coal is the lifeblood of Witbank.

Those who are too poor to buy coal from Mr Skhosana's donkey cart pick up the coal that falls from the overloaded goods train that chugs its way to Ogies and Minnaar via the East Rand and to the Johannesburg mines. We can afford to buy it from the man with the donkey cart. He sits in the front holding the reins, with his two teenage sons in the back ready to serve his customers.

We learn to check the hessian bags, selecting those that are pointy from the outlines of the coal pieces and rejecting the rounded bags that are filled with coal dust. We have already heard him howling '*Malahle!*'(Coal!) from the top of the street. That is, if Ouma Sussie has not sent my cousin Wincie or Miriam to tell her sister that Baba Skhosana is on his way. Ouma lets me wait at the gate with the money to pay him. His two sons never seem to have anything to say. Each drags a bag to the edge of the cart, jumps off and bends down as if to kneel, then slides it over the head onto the back and, without pausing, walks in a trot to the coal shed. The path to the backyard is a straight line along the house wall, leading directly to the lavatory, which is directly opposite the gate. Diagonally from the corner of the wall is the half-walled coal shed, past the two adjacent rooms, with flower beds, one of which is Uncle Bower's. After my uncle leaves our home, his room remains locked and Ouma will not allow anyone to enter it.

One after the other, they hurl the heavy bags over the low wall of the shed and pause before untying them. Then they hold each bag by the corners and pour out the coal. A quick-rising cloud of black dust is a sign that the coal is of a low grade; at times it is wet and glistens in the sunlight and we have to wait for the sun to dry it. Rarely is the coal shiny and clean. If Ouma is watching from the low kitchen window she rushes into the street to complain to the seller. But whatever the exchange between them, it ends in friendly resignation, as neither has the power to change anything. He is softly spoken, and when Ouma complains he just nods. 'I hear you,' he responds. *Ngiyezwa*. It disarms her. She shrugs her shoulders and walks back into the house.

Meanwhile, the two sweaty young men drink from tins of water we have cooled under the massive apricot tree, which shades the chicken coop. They drink deeply, and without as much as a smile they retrace their steps back to the donkey cart. They are raggedly dressed and the soft dust of soot from their clothes draws a jagged line back to the donkey cart. All you can see in their faces is their teeth and their weary eyes. If there is a pot of mielie cobs on the stove, or the apricots are ripe, I hand over the money and the food in a brown paper or newspaper parcel. Maybe the coal cost one shilling and a sixpence, or two and six, I don't remember, but Baba Skhosana counts it studiously before serving the next customer or going on his way.

THERE IS a little dance ditty we compose as children. It is full of joy and holds a special meaning to me. In my own solitude, it still rouses a longing for the romance of childhood.

Throughout our lives all I have had to do to make my brother laugh is swing my waist and hold my arms akimbo and chant,

'Aaja Jwi, Jwo Ju!' It is fun and affectionate merriment, a testimony of our innocent love. That is what we do, out of Ouma's earshot or when we dandle my little sister, Elaine, when she is a baby We also dance it, hands aloft, feet stomping when a tickled victim, drunk with laughter, lies, head curled in to cover the vulnerable cusp of the neck, laying bare the armpits where little waving fingers wrest even more drunken merriment.

In Witbank the word 'love' is never loosely thrown about. Given names are retired soon after baptism to be resurrected on formal occasions, like the morning assembly at school when you have to shout out, 'Present,' or the group chorus sings out, 'Absent.' Or at the formal ceremonies of the church and the law or at funerals when the one whose name is called out can no longer answer back. To this day it breaks my guard down when someone calls me Babsie. It is an announcement of an intimacy beyond the confines of boarding school, or the public platforms of panel discussions on this or that historical crime when the women and the children are tethered to each other, folded and filed away on a forgotten shelf like an inconvenient truth that does not fit the narrative. KwaGuqa is where I learn that my mind can create fantasies that belong to me alone, and where I can play out roles to fit the demands of my own needs.

'Babsie' denotes the time when I come to realise that I am something more than a charge to Ouma. It is an embrace, a quick stroke on the side of my arm, something that defines a singular affinity to her, which 'Barbara' can never achieve. Or that outstanding occasion when she adds '*my meisiekind*' (my girl child) to her 'Babsie'.

My grandmother talks a lot about heart. According to her the most intense feelings are congregated at the cusp of the heart where transparently there is the least room. Thus she calls Hugh '*my hart se punt*' (the tip, or cusp, of my heart). He is her first grandchild, the fruit of my mother's virginity that Ouma guarded until my mother's wedding night. He, a male child, is the one who will make up for all the broken promises that have landed her here in KwaGuqa. She regrets that he has nothing of Walter Bower in his physical features, neither the colour of his skin nor the shape of his nose. He is a true Masekela, something she pronounced with an air of regret. Her daughter, another *hart se punt*, is the receptacle that has reproduced for the Masekelas a replica of their powerful strain that has admitted not even an atom of the Mabenas or the Bowers.

My grandmother is a stern and often angry person. Her motto is not to go too far, to stay within the bounds of propriety. She leaves anecdotes hanging on the branches of present actualities. She keeps a keen eye on her clients and rarely takes part in their conversations unless they veer into the political or sexual sphere. But when Malan leads the election campaign of 1947 for the National Party, his speeches stir more memories that were repressed during the small interval before World War II.

When the men become animated by her brew and the conversation turns to the daily slights and cuts of life at their workplace in the mines, she falls back on her assertion that the power of the white man is in evidence everywhere. Did they not build machines that could fly in the sky? Could they not trap light and turn it on with a switch, and what of their ships that could sail on the waters? Yes, Eiselen was a hard man, and his visits to the Middelburg Mission Station instilled fear and anxiety in the refugees who had fled to Botshabelo and exiled themselves to the mission station in desperation. And was it not the son of the same Eiselen who was now the secretary to this very Malan, who was now forcing open their fingers, bending them with force, to wrest their last earned mite to fling on the heaps of lucre so as to uplift their kith and kin, many of whom could not even read and write? They may call it by a new name, apartheid, but it is the same, the same colour bar that squeezed them off their land and hurled them onto the mission stations, only to end up on work gangs on the very land they once owned and underneath the earth to mine coal.

No one dares to argue with her. It is her house, her liquor they have chosen to drink, and her rules to be obeyed. Apart from that, theirs is to steal some joy from the drinks they have come to buy and rush back to the mine compound before the gates close at 9:00 p.m.

As a child, my mother seems to have been spared the many tasks that are assigned to me by Ouma and I am persuaded that this was due in great part to the way she looked, a half-white young girl growing up in the African section of KwaGuqa. Her skin is much paler than my Uncle Bower's. The best is when she washes her hair in the portable zinc basin. I like to pour the warm water from the jug to rinse the suds from her long, black, smooth hair, which she enfolds in a clean towel to dry. It's the most perfect time when I watch her comb her hair, holding it up close to the skull with her left hand and forcing the comb through the tangled bunch of hair at the top with her right hand, then letting it fall back on her shoulder, a mass of unruly black curls just short of silky. It is a private ritual between the two of us. 'And now you can help me,' she says as she hands me the brush. It is the only time that her hair is displayed freely and the secret of its abundant wilfulness will soon be concealed in a long plait on each side, modestly tucked and pinned together at the back of her head. Too soon her weekend visit comes to a close, pitching me into a pit of gloom, bereft.

On her visits the front room is opened up and we sit there playing Snakes and Ladders and card games when she is not teaching me how to read and write. In between, visitors drop in to greet the visitor from Johannesburg and, mostly in isiNdebele, she repeats the answers to the questions that abound about the breadth and the depth of the City of Gold, its mine dumps, *izindunduma*, from which few can find their way back home: One, 'Last seen in Benoni,' 'Heard to have moved to Brakpan.'

Another, 'Now living in Germiston, still working for the same white people who took him with them when they were transferred to head office.'

Yet another one, 'Still in jail for getting into a fight with the supervisor who took over from Edwards.'

'Yebo, things are getting harder for black people under the new order. People are scattered just like chaff.'

'Ee yah, this land is becoming the Canaan of the whites. Mmmh, what can we say.'

And my mother, always responding, 'The only hope for us is in learning. We must encourage the young ones to better their education. It is the only hope we have.'

My mother, like many of her peers who have gone to school, is trained to be a teacher. She married my father on the condition that she would continue to pursue her studies. From the time of their marriage, my father held a day job and sculpted at night. In between, he studied through correspondence courses to become a health inspector. He could never have kept his promise to pay towards my mother's further education. But he could not prevent Ouma from paying for her studies. He was already indebted to her, having not had the means to make the expected lobola when they got married. When she is irritated, Ouma sings the song of how he still owes her.

Dr Ray Phillips, an American missionary, and his wife, Dora, established the Jan H Hofmeyr School of Social Work in Johannesburg to train Africans in a profession that had until then been the preserve of whites. Living in City Deep, where my father had started off as a mine policeman and graduated to a mine clerk, my mother heard of this new school and Ouma rallied to her support. With the active support of my father's two sisters Johanna and Clara, who cherished Ouma, and his youngest brother Kenneth, who became her closest ally, and after a number of heated arguments and debates within the Masekela family, Ouma stepped in and my mother became a student again, completing her diploma in social work with 'flying colours', as my father would say. With hindsight I can imagine the awkward position in which this placed my father: how to explain to his Northern conservative father that his young wife of dubious origins, not Tlokwa, drops off a Masekela heir at her Ndebele mother's house, which is a tavern, so that she can leave her home every day to go to school with men in town. Worse, that his mother-in-law is making a financial contribution to this household.

It was not remarked upon openly, but my mother did not come from an orthodox African family like my father. We lived in an African township and no one found it strange that we spoke Afrikaans at home and it was no special achievement that we spoke perfect isiNdebele as well. But English was another matter altogether. She had been raised in a single-parent family while her father, reputed to be a Scottish sporting man, lived in Johannesburg with another woman who bore him two boys, my uncles Victor and Boetie.

Until I return – years later, as an adult – to South Africa, my focus is always on wanting to be somewhere other than where I find myself. Far away from KwaGuqa, in Accra and in London, in New York and in Lusaka, I was to spend twenty-seven years remaking the haunts of my childhood and embellishing the past to fit the future.

It is not until September 1990 that I see Johanna again, still stout but bent and ninety-nine years old, sitting next to the coal stove in the kitchen of her house in Ennerdale, overrun by grandchildren and great-grandchildren. Coming home without my mother – Mama Atshi, as I called her – to say my name is like replaying her death. It turns me into a howling child. Mama Atshi gone, dead from an oncoming goods train, stuck on the railroad track in her bakkie.

✤ ✤ ✤

WHEN IT is time to leave KwaGuqa and Ouma sells her stand at number 76 Tollman Street, most of her belongings and all of her chickens, and we count the money to find that she has accumulated over five hundred pounds and she swears me to silence never to reveal her worth to anyone, especially my father, she says she will keep the money until she can find a piece of land to build herself a small house of her own.

'I cannot live under another man's roof,' she grumbles. 'I am my own boss. I have always been my own boss and I raised and educated my children. It is these hands that have raised his children.'

I am accustomed to this soliloquy. It does not disturb me. Ouma felt put upon. It was too much. She raised Minkie and as soon as he could run errands for her they took him away. Just when he was old enough to be of help to her. Her son Khalo has already been wrested from her by that Mira temptress Tillie, who was not ashamed to steal into his bed on Ouma's property. The Miras poisoned his brain. The only one she has left is Pannie, my mother. But when she goes on a rant like this, I have learnt not to take offence or to be concerned. I am nearly twelve and over the years we have grown close in our own way.

It is decades later that I begin to understand why anger, longing, resentment and death were the forces that drove us closer together. When she put the lid on my curiosity she shut me into an incompleteness, a bane that, over time, became a great motivator. As I look back now, I see how that need to know spurred me on.

And I glory in the secrets she kept from me, secrets I had to seek out for myself.

TWO

UNCLE BOWER
AND THE MEN OF WITBANK

WE ARE taught to call him Uncle Bower. He is my mother's elder brother and the two of them are Ouma's only children. I am too young to understand why but it is Ouma Sussie who likes to dig up the past, breaching the reticence that is upheld so strictly by Johanna. They are as different in stature as they are in temperament. Ouma Sussie is tall, and would have been a perfect fit for the traditional brass rings worn as neck chokers and leg and arm bands by married Ndebele women. Her sister Ouma Johanna is barely five feet tall, squat and firm in comparison.

Sussie walks slowly and warily with a cane because her legs have burnt from inside, as they say. As soon as we see her ambling towards our house, I run to the front room to ready the footstool for her. The flames from the internal combustion are displayed in a discolouration of faded pink on the front of her legs.

Even inside the house, Johanna never walks slowly. She is always in a hurry and is suspicious of people strolling. She marches and races on her short legs, cleaning up dirt. The lasting image in my mind is of her trotting just before dark with the four-gallon tin of beer on her head, speeding to get home to strain the beer before her customers arrive.

I think her only friend is Ouma Sussie. It is one of the one thousand reasons why she hates Mira. It was after his snitching that Ouma Sussie was arrested, and when she came out of jail she never fully regained the use of her legs. Ouma Sussie scours the past to revisit their youth and now and again she succeeds in coaxing Johanna to remember what she would have rather forgotten. With Ouma Sussie there, it is soothing to hear the laughing that sometimes brings tears to their eyes. It is quiet in the late afternoon, unless one of the cocks jumps on a hen and has his way. This show of force draws a chorus of clucking from the rest of the hens, who jump up high to guard their downy chicks in their nests, clucking loudly in chorus, raising the alarm as if daring the rooster to try them. No one owns a car on our street and the only other noise is the steaming goods train hooting into the silence, the choo-choo train so beloved by my brother. There is also the siren from the colliery that goes off at the same time every day. When it sounds unexpectedly at a different time, everybody comes out of their houses with worried faces, wondering about the men they know and the men they do not know from Malawi, Mozambique, Lesotho, Zambia, Swaziland, all working underground in the Witbank Colliery.

When you walk from town, down KwaGuqa's main road, past the Indian section where the Asian vendors have their homes behind their shops, on the single bus route to the colliery, you reach a crossing at Tollman Street, our street, where there are two churches facing each other. With its dark brickwork, the Lutheran Church looks like an old barn with a peaked roof, while opposite it, facing the colliery, is the whitewashed Bantu Methodist Church, which we call the Donkey Church. One of the first fruits of the African Independent Church movement, it is living proof of the rejection of the white domination of the Wesleyan Church. (I can't recall its location now, but there was also the Ethiopian Church, whose members wore colourful costumes.)

If you turn left, you walk down towards the stream that borders the location. The last house on the right is that of the gogo who is the official ear-piercer for the girl children in our part of the location. We all go to her when we are about to enter primary school, and the whole operation is carried out under the shade of the peach tree next to her house. It is our first test of stoicism. I go there with my cousin Wincie, accompanied by our granny sisters, who have been preparing us for the ordeal. We have been told, You either sit still and endure or you squirm like a worm and have your ear ripped into pieces.

The surgeon, Ouma Mnisi, is well known for her skill, and our mothers and aunts all have working ear piercings to show for it. In the days before our procedure, stories abound about the exemplary behaviour of our aunts and our mothers when their ears were pierced. They sat still without a whimper, just squeezing hard on a supportive hand. We want to be like them. We await their next visit so that we can tell the story told of how bravely we too faced the piercing.

The surgery is sharp and quick but the penetration of the threaded needle through the skin of the earlobe is like a tear in the pit of the stomach, like falling off an abyss with closed eyes and miraculously landing in icy-cold water alive. The ensuing days of healing, in which the possibility of the thread catching on some object, getting hooked and tearing through the skin of the lobe, divorce us from everyone. The thick black cotton thread is knotted to stay in place and it hangs loosely but close to the ear, like a temporary earing. Every day after the operation I sit still on the chair to undergo the exercise of moving the thread after the cleansing with small balls of cotton wool dipped in boiled water with some drops of Dettol. Then Ouma applies some yellow Blue Seal Vaseline to help the healing and keep the skin from drying up and crusting.

The after-pain of piercing the ears is the first lesson we girls have on how to keep a distance from others, guarding the physical space around our bodies so that nothing, even the caress of the softest feather, could come near that lobe with the burning fire inside the forming hole. When the wound heals, there is a private ceremony when the simple, thin, nine-carat gold bands are guided through the new holes and we parade around as young girls with earrings. It seems sudden, how one morning you discover you can touch your ear without pain.

But each Easter or Christmas, when we go to the cemetery with our Johannesburg visitors in tow and our solemn grannies, all made up with faraway looks, the sight of Ouma Mnisi's house is a reminder that pain is not like the air you breathe but an occurrence that comes and goes, or settles down, quietly finding a place with other memories in a pit somewhere in the bottom of your belly. But up in an aeroplane if there is turbulence, or in a nightmare when I scream and there is no voice or I run and there is no motion, I feel it there. It is a sleeping fright that never goes away and controlling it is growing up.

I have known some folks who never knew that dread.

Walking back up the street from the cemetery, we pass the houses that are different from one another except for their painted zinc roofs with gutters that lead the water through pipes into a barrel or a bucket, or even a water tank on the side of the wall, if you are a rare bird with the means. Rainwater is believed to be soft but the elders agree that the best-flavoured water comes from the well. No single house has everything, and a gift of clean rainwater or some water from a well in a clay gourd is deeply appreciated, its sweetness much dissected and contrasted to waters from earlier climes and former regions of habitation.

Similarly, there is a great deal of talk about the quality of home-made ginger beer, dumplings and *soetkoekies* (spiced biscuits).

Reputations are made and broken over the talent or lack thereof in producing these items and, for weeks after a funeral or a wedding, talk persists about the disappearing art of cuisine. Almost all homes have a fruit tree, a chimney and a food garden. Very few keep flower gardens. But even from the bottom of the street the toy spires of the two churches are visible, as is the hulking almost-ruin of Mira's palace of joy, which obscures Sussie's corner house.

Ouma keeps very close to home. We go only to Ouma Sussie's, church, the store, or to fetch water from the communal tap or to attend to the burying or retrieving of the four-gallon tins fermenting in the holes in the veld above the street. Going to the cemetery is a big adventure.

On the way up Tollman Street we hardly stop to speak, except when one of the grannies calls back, returning a neighbour's greeting. Our next-door neighbour is a widow and reticent like Ouma. Her two daughters work and live in one of the towns on the Reef. When she and Ouma speak over the fence it is about their mielie patches, the size of their pumpkins and tomatoes, and the weather. Unlike the people in our extended family, this neighbour and her daughters have only come to KwaGuqa recently, long after my mother's marriage and move to Johannesburg. My mother who, despite Ouma's protests, visits everyone she knows when she comes to KwaGuqa does not even know them. They are not from Middelburg and only speak siSwati.

The pleasantries they exchange aside, they have never entered each other's houses. It is the same with the neighbours behind us. They are related to the Reverend Abraham Serote, who died in 1930 and was one of the team who translated the Bible into Sepedi – Northern Sotho. Gerard Sekoto, the famous South African painter who died in Paris, is a sometime visitor to his aunt, and he met my mother just before my parents married. (I have never fantasised about what would have happened if he had married my mother. But I loved meeting him in Paris in 1964. His eyes lit up when I said that Pauline Bower was my mother, and he remembered her beauty.) He would never have been an acceptable suitor for Ouma's daughter, just as my father could never have been, although he did succeed in marrying Mama in 1938. There is a small cameo of my mother drawn in pencil that Sekoto presented to her once when he was visiting. Apparently, as everyone was laughing and talking he was quietly drawing my mother's face, and presented the drawing to her as he left.

It is one of those things that fade in the reality of life. The portrait, drawn in pencil on a piece of cardboard, disappears, and is only remembered when Sekoto is in the news again decades later.

Those who come to Ouma's home enter through the front gate and are usually family, historical friends or drinking clients A knock on the front door could only mean one of two things: the police or a dreaded messenger with a telegram from the post office.

When they are on a visit to Ouma's house, the young women next door ask if they can take me with them to go and gather wood in the forest. I am about eight then and not the only girl child taken along for the adventure – my cousin Wincie, about nine, comes too. As is the way, the group consists of females only, ranging from teenagers to these two women neighbours who are in their twenties but have clearly been raised in the rural areas. We leave early in the morning and pass through the veld where I recognise the place where we buried our latest brew. I have never walked this far into the veld but I feel very protected in the company of these women, who are at ease and unafraid in the veld. We go deep into the silent forest, to an area where the wood is dry and you can snap off the drying branches. Here, most of the trees are half-dead. For some inexplicable reason some of the trees still have a few green leaves on their meagre branches, but all around, lying randomly, are dried-up branches ready for the taking. The women make long bundles and help us little girls to put together the shorter bundles mainly of slender branches fit for kindling, and not too heavy for our heads. They help us to tie our bundles with rope, which each of us has brought along, and then they put on our heads the round cotton scarf doughnut that protects our scalps, and then we all make the journey back home.

We avoid the path with the small open pits, some of them still emitting smoke from long-smouldering fires underground. There are no signs or warnings announcing these sudden small pits and all around the earth is charred grey and our feet are hot from the ground. Our bundles of firewood on our heads, we walk in single file behind the sharp-eyed guide in front, a woman familiar with the path home. Wincie and I perform admirably and for the rest of the week we bask in the praise of our young-womanly achievement as the kindling we have gathered fires up the coals in the Welcome Dovers. We are becoming proper young women, useful to our hardworking grandmothers, they tell us. We beam.

As usual I am too graphic in my descriptions of the day in the forest. The next time there is a wood-gathering exercise Ouma insists on coming along. She is horrified. On our return Ouma announces that I will not be going back as it is too dangerous. She is shocked by the hazardous pathways and swears she will never again expose me to so much danger. 'What would I say to Thomas if something happens to you?' she asks. It is the beginning of a pattern for the future as increasingly it seems that anything that brings me joy is deemed unsuitable and dangerous and summarily forbidden.

Just before everybody arrives for the Christmas holidays, the two young women next door are arrested and charged with the killing of a young black man. He interfered with them, it is said. They were together, walking home near the woods in the gathering darkness. Their lift in the van from Middelburg was late and the town was deserted when they arrived. It was not safe for women alone at night, from the police and from all men. They only noticed they were being followed when he was almost upon them. He interfered with them and they fought back. They did not stop hitting him, even when he was down. They were angry and they stoned him with rocks and bricks until he went still. It is a big court case and at night the drinking men give their received version of the live testimony. There is some hush-hush about the details of the outrage perpetrated by the deceased but his facial features have been so distorted by the assault that he is unrecognisable to his next of kin, one of the clients. He interfered with the sisters and they have their torn clothes as evidence.

Hawu!

They overpowered him.

This has never happened in the history of KwaGuqa.

It is not natural for women to overpower a man and kill him.

They show no remorse.

They stare straight back at the people in the courtroom, without shame.

It is all consternation, especially from Ouma's clients. It was not done in stealth, nothing like slow poisoning, something women are deemed capable of. And the young women are unapologetic, pleading not guilty. No sackcloth and ashes for them; they wear their best Johannesburg fashion clothes for their court appearances.

One day I get a quick glance of them from behind Ouma's lace curtain. It is on the day that they are given a suspended sentence. They have won the case and they leave KwaGuqa in the middle of the night without saying goodbye. Later on Ouma swears that it had all been an omen of what was to come and change our lives to the point of our own departure from KwaGuqa.

✧ ✧ ✧

NOT LONG afterwards my mother writes a letter telling Ouma about Khalo. He is coming to KwaGuqa for a football match against his old team, the Witbank Aces. The team will be rushing back to Brakpan after the match but she hopes he will have time to pass by quickly to pay his respects. Would he be welcome to stop and greet on his way out? The visit would be in four weeks.

Old people seem to repeat the same stories over and over again, going back over the same ground and seemingly returning to confirm what they already know, with a sigh. There is so much not to forget and much of it has already happened. I want to know it all. By the time I am ten years old I have learnt that there are many more stories lurking around the one being told. The horrible incident that occurred between Ouma and Uncle Bower is not mentioned. But Mira is always there, an unwanted fixture three doors away, leaning over the wall of the crooked, rotting veranda wall of his wrecked mansion. He has questions I am forbidden to answer and oh, the quandary of avoiding rudeness to an elderly person versus the fear of punishment if caught out in conversation with the devil himself! Although Ouma and I do not refer to it directly it is something we share, the blood, the tears, the anger, the tattered clothing, the shouting, the screams and the curses, all a departure from our everyday routine that is designed to eschew attention from outsiders.

In fact, that episode rescues me from the exile of childhood into the realm of adult fellowship with my grandmother. Now there is something I have been involved in that no adult can mention in my presence. Not even Auntie Tinnie!

Now Khalo is coming back to play a football match. Will he come to his mother's house or does he still hold anger towards her for hating Tilly so much that she almost destroyed him, her own son?

Ouma keeps the letter in the pocket of her *voorskoot*. Several times, I watched her sit down to re-read it. In the bedroom, at the kitchen table, she reads it but she says nothing to me. This time her eyes are not failing her. She does not ask me to read it for her. It goes back into the pocket. When she nearly trips on the small step at the kitchen door she screams out my name. 'Babsie, I almost fell,' she says. 'It's this letter,' she says as she reaches for her pocket. The three handwritten pages scatter on the ground outside the door. 'It's Khalo,' she says. 'He is coming back. Go and call your Ouma Sussie.'

MY GRANNIES are sisters closed up and bound together in a past that was engulfed in an alien greed for land, for labour and for overall domination that negated every human aspiration to a life of dignity for Africans. But worse is the story that is untold, of female people like them born into an unforgiving triumphalism, to remain victims of a patriarchy joined to a colonial conquest, unabashedly racist and equally paternalistic to its females. They played the unsung role that guaranteed the emergence of every new generation since the first white man found his feet on African soil. They are the great secret of history, and have enjoyed the least attention for their supreme exercise in survival.

It is they who have borne the burden of regeneration that has brought us all here. They may not have heard of Sarah Baartmaan or of Krotoa, Eva van Meerhof. Perhaps they heard in passing of her majesty Modjadji the Rain Queen, or of Mmanthatisi the

Warrior Queen of Batlokwa. Because all the noise was about Nongqawuse. She took centre stage in the tales that the white men wrote about unconverted natives. Riddled by a religion that did not practise what it preached, saddled on a horse gone berserk, women like my grannies rode the beast of uncertainty holding fast to the reins, uncertain how many legs the horse would raise to shake off the rider. From the earliest encounters with the would-be moguls, the spice merchants of Portugal, and on to their rivals from Batavia, these foremothers of South Africa made their noble contribution to our survival. From those earliest encounters, they were branded by a self-serving religious ethos designed to justify anything that could have been an obstacle in the way of the colonists. It was the power held by all men, un-equal as it was between master and servant, that they withstood and which made it possible for all of us to be here today.

Much of the focus of South African history is on the actions of the European protagonists, the minority Germans and French who were easily assimilated by the predominant Dutch and British Cape colonists. The indigenes are treated as a hindrance and a nuisance. Were it not for the Bambathas, Moshoeshoes, Sekhukhunes and Mabhogos, who resisted conquest to the last, Africans would have been remembered, if at all, as a mere back-drop to an unoccupied, gorgeous, virgin landscape just waiting to be ravaged by heroic pioneers. From the early days of the expansion of European settlement, the indigenes inhabiting the land on the different routes neighbouring the Cape Colony had been considered an impediment to the grand schemes of those at the helm of political power. Their schemes of expan-sion and sovereignty were predicated upon the presumption that they had a right to get what they wanted, and they tended to resort to force when the negotiations did not go their way. They would not understand that the power of the chief resided in his custodianship of the land he held in trust for the entire polity.

Ultimately, their definition of the inhabitants of the land as less than human legitimised the so-called civilising mission in which the missionaries played a divided role. As we observe the first encounters between the Boers and the Ndebeles, according to the records of missionaries, traders and government officials, we note that at first there is some semblance of acknowledgement of the authority of the chiefs. Their land is progressively appropriated by the first Trekker Boers from the Cape with the tacit agency of the ZAR and the British Crown. What they consider as voluntary gifts to the new inhabitants is interpreted as tribute by the strangers. In the economic rivalries and competition between the ZAR and the British that led to the first war between the British and the slave-owning Dutch farmers and for all subsequent skirmishes, Africans fall into the role of incidental proxies, sometimes even settling stale vendettas with erstwhile rivals for the benefit of the invaders. By the end of the second Anglo-Boer War my grannies are already attached to Dutch households as child domestic servants. It was from that kitchen window that Ouma, barely a teenager, saw the dirt-poor Boer children emerging ragged from their wagon to the sound of the muffled cry of a newborn baby.

The Africans fought on both sides of the war and, as was already the established custom in South Africa, their contribution to either side was never measured or weighed, least of all compensated. After the war, when the Union of South Africa was formed, the peace that was forged totally excluded them. Three years later their fate was sealed with the 1913 Land Act, which forced them into becoming unskilled labourers in the mining industry unless they moved to the overcrowded Native reserves where they could become spectators to the starvation of their landless families in an environment of rife unemployment and

cruel demands for hut tax. They were denuded of every semblance of citizenship and reduced to itinerant labourers, forever
in search of a permanent place to call home. They were now the
third and fourth generation of the converted in one of Merensky's
thirty-six mission stations. What had been the heartland of their
nation became a territory where summary eviction on pain
of death, forced labour and enslavement were commonplace.
Neighbours, friends, families were scattered across the land. What
remained were renamed places and hearsay about who had wandered where. Their oral narratives were muted by the scrawls in
the personal diaries of missionaries, petty officials and adventurers, written to justify and exonerate the authors, who saw their
subjects only as props in a story of preconceived notions.

For all the grannies, nostalgia drips blood. The early past is
rarely referred to and the meagre snatches of remembered episodes of racial abuse and brutality are summarily halted when we
children walk into the room. So, we learn how to listen without
being caught. We become detectives in search of what they have
lost – this is no longer tangible but it hangs about in the curtness
of their answers and the softness of the cheap cuts of meat they
boil then brown with onions for gravy. Their conversations are
meagre, interposed with recitals of the quality of their sleep, who
of the dead visited them in last night's dream, our behaviour,
white men and the weather. They create riddles that are yet unravelling and still confounding. Their memories are cut-up heart
strips, Humpty Dumpty pieces they do not want to put together
again. What they have seen, felt and heard is unspeakable.

Now, their hearts are set only on the imperative of our formal
education. So, they push us firmly into schooling, hoping we too
will be powerful like those who have stripped them of everything. They laugh as if they are crying, swallow their tears and
wipe their eyes with the backs of their hands. They fish out their

handkerchiefs, rags from discarded clothing, blow their noses and shout out commands. Our faces have to be cleaned of snot and the traces of our pap and *vleis* (meat) meals. The meat is bought at Baba George Mafuyana's butchery and he makes sure to add a *bonsella* (bonus) of bones that we suck and chew to small particles and spit out onto the side of the plate. We relish sucking out the marrow of the bones and learn at an early age not to choke on it. It is not unusual for an adult to retrieve an unfinished bone from a child's plate in order to suck it again. We are taught not to waste and never to boast about the food we have eaten. It may have been missionary training not to waste but our grannies are familiar with hunger, as were those who raised them to be servants and slaves.

Out of their hearing, we sing, repeatedly, exulting in the freedom of saying the name of an adult without the honorary prefix of respect expected from children for their elders:

Georgie Mafuyana, *inyama yakho iyadura* (Georgie Mafuyana, your meat is costly).

Mr George Mafuyana was not born in Witbank, nor was Oupa Legwale, nor Father Dlephu, nor Principal Monnakgotla. Our grannies and everyone else under the age of fifty-five are from somewhere else. KwaGuqa is a town of migrants and Witbank with its coal mines is the magnet.

It is the time of the looming apartheid, the offspring of the *khalabhayi* (colour bar). Malan! Malan! His name is everywhere in the newspaper and I read the news aloud to Ouma's clients about the native problem that is us.

❖❖❖

THERE ARE no vistas surrounding Witbank Location. None of the mountains, waterfalls or gurgling brooks that I read about in the fairy tale books that my parents bring me. At the top of the slight incline towards the railway line is the main street, which is our border with the open, flat grassland. A few hundred metres ahead is the railway line for the goods train that carries the coal to Johannesburg and further to the port of Lourenço Marques. Beyond is the wooded area where young women collect firewood. Often, some of the poorest, old and young, wait until the echo of the steam engine has waned, to swoop out of the waving grass and collect the coals that have fallen from the high-piled carriages. The gatherers work fast because loitering around this snaking key point of coal capital is strictly forbidden. Legend among us children is that if you placed a needle on the tracks it could derail the whole train, but we do not try it because we fear being taken away and never seen again. We have heard people speak of so many they have known but never seen again. Disappearance is a familiarity we fear most, and no matter how often it happens we never grow accustomed to it.

My lasting impression of KwaGuqa is of boundless, cloudless blue skies, and from the first I am haunted by the question of where the horizon ends. It is most frustrating that it is always moving, when it actually seems like a giant canopy from which my father, my mother and my brother are excluded when he goes back to live with them. It is an enclosure that can change character and spew hailstorms, thunder and lightning, and occasional snow. Worse still, on occasion it brings swarms of locusts, and sudden tornadoes that flatten the shacks of the squatter people in Schoongezicht. The houses I know in our location have strong foundations and roofs with ceilings. We have windows and curtains and thick brick-and-concrete walls and doors with keys because Johanna made sure to build a strong house when she came back from the diamond fields of Kimberley. We do not know anyone who has set eyes on the vastness of the ocean.

We hear that it swallowed up the warship *SS Mendi*, with hundreds of African men who had been enlisted to serve behind the lines as labourers and then rewarded with nothing. My granny sisters know at least three men who drowned in the icy cold waters. They say that was the reason why the daughter of the old woman who pierced our ears never married: the man she had promised to marry went down with the *Mendi*. Even Ouma, who knows Lydenburg and Barberton, old gold mining areas, who went to the diamond fields of Kimberley to look for Walter, leaving Mama with Ouma Sussie, has never seen the sea. I cannot with my child's mind divine the sea except for its vast, moving power, and when I place it underneath the moving horizons of KwaGuqa it becomes a gargantuan formless mass taking away my breath. There is little of the landscape that I remember of Witbank, except the open forever skies with occasional cotton-fluffy white clouds. We have sharp disagreements about the artwork in the sky, arguing about the resemblance of the objects in the heavens to the humans and animals we see every day. Even as we argue the skyscapes change and wisp into new momentary formations. Occasionally a lone aeroplane drones across the sky and sends us into a frenzy of chanting, 'Aeroplane! Aeroplane! Aeroplane!' Our plaintive cries, unbeknownst to us, are unheard by the men in the flying machines. They are like the centuries-old unanswered appeals to the authorities of our gone country.

It is the tall, undulating grass that I recall clearly, which makes my eyes smart on a visit to California in 1973, as does the red clay I see in North Carolina when I visit Willie Kgositsile there some years later. It is like the first time I travel from Lusaka to Zimbabwe by car. The sight of the bluegum trees standing tall near the sculptural rocks, some standing high and slender, others plump and reclining precariously on top of each other in the colours of straw and red mud mixed together, awakens a grievous native longing for the country I persist in calling home, the one which, after more than twenty years of rupture, I now only know from anti-apartheid statistical records.

These 'surplus people', so poignantly and unforgettably described by Phyllis Ntantala-Jordan in her essay 'Widows of the Reserves', my fellow citizens, the majority forcibly removed to arid lands, in the land of plenty, with multitudes of starving infants barely strong enough to whimper and soon interred in the graves of Dimbaza or QwaQwa or Gazankulu, now only remembered by an empty plastic feeding bottle on the teeny dusty mound. These widows, their only companions the ragged children with eloquent eyes speaking the language of hunger with a precision so sharp, slicing straight through the gnarled, the haggard, the old and the infirm, thrown on the rubbish heap of uselessness, unable to slave in the industrial fields, the 'widows of the reserves' so piercingly drawn burying the infants whose lives were counted in days, watching the sky for the rains that never come, hungering for the quickening touch to release all the waters.

The genuflecting grasses, bowing low in the veld above KwaGuqa, seem to dance of their own accord, rising and falling to the tune of the breeze. On cold winter mornings they stand stiff and straight, white with frost, the still-rising sun about to tear them into drops of diamond ice.

But it is the unseen body of waters that swept away hundreds and hundreds of surprised men who could not swim that lingers forever in my mind. There are two things I fear most at that time: empty spaces and the sea. But when Uncle Bower is gone, it is the empty quiet that rushes my heart. I feel safer when Ouma is there with me. The open landscapes of my country hide the hideous deeds committed under its skies. If God is everywhere, I wonder why he does not stop the sinners and, worse still, why they are not afraid to carry out their evil deeds.

✦ ✦ ✦

IT IS the dread of a hopeless life, tethered to the whims and fancies of the powerful people who have subjugated them, that propels them to KwaGuqa. They have come to Witbank because they had to. They are migrants who yearn for their own windows and doors to open and to close as they wish, who hope perhaps to have a small yard where they can keep a few chickens and maybe a fruit tree that will yield enough for them to make some jam for the winter months. Staying there means that every day they are reminded of how they have been brought down.

What brought my grannies to KwaGuqa was their rejection of the abject hardships imposed on them by those they feared and despised, and the belief that anything was better than serf-dom. Conquest has not robbed them of the ability to listen, to observe the changes in the world around them and to imagine the possibility of something different for themselves. They have some acquaintance with Asian traders, whom they refer to as amaSuluman, and have interacted with Africans from Mozam-bique, Bechuanaland, Basutoland, Swaziland, Malawi and other neighbouring countries in the British colonies, so they are not strangers to the phenomenon of migration, especially as the de-velopment of coal, gold and diamond mines brings forth a new world of enterprise and a novel social order, somewhat different from the racial and religious hierarchy in which they have been raised. Racism still abounds but the surprise of discovering prodigious amounts of minerals while acquiring quick wealth has not yet lent itself to a concerted effort towards systematic racial legislation. Above all, the labour of the Africans is the main concern at the time. These are frontier towns, where laws are made as the situation arises. It is here, then, in these new towns, that people like my grannies think they might earn some dignity in the long run, some respite from a grovelling rural life, which they have grown to abhor.

It cannot have been an easy story to tell us, their grandchildren. When they recall stories about Khalo's childhood, one of them would close by exclaiming his name out loud, almost as if they still cannot believe what they remember of him or even that it was better not to visit that place again. Kha – lo! *Ja, wragtig!* (Yes, truly!)

Serving tea to my oumas is a rich field of information. Intent on not spilling a drop onto the saucers I carry myself with calm, belying my concentration on gathering yet more clues to solve the puzzles of our family's adults. What they did not say somehow mingles with the new titbits, cues and fragments collected from my other eavesdropping sessions. A useful dab of some colour here with a small splash of detail there, put together while holding out the sugar basin and handing over the warmed milk, dawdling back to the kitchen to get the tin of home-baked cookies from the kitchen – all these moves were planned with precision to coincide with whatever moments of truth were forthcoming. In this way I put together the saga of their lives shifted by detours and lurking reversals causing damned pauses. Uncle Bower's is one such pause. His church name is Solomon and it is only his football fans who shout it out when he scores goal after goal on the soccer field.

The resurrecting of my upbringing defies sequence and is dominated by fading portraits, half-lit by flames of flickering candlelight and pointing fingers. We have no family archive, only a few faded, terse official documents mostly noting DOB, DOD, race and town. There are also faded pictures, some of whose corners have been gnawed away by the little teeth of fieldmice who found their way into the moth-eaten cardboard boxes that are exiled on the top of Ouma's wardrobe in our bedroom next to the kitchen. It is in that little room where, listening from my iron bed with a coir mattress, I can hear the noises of the last stragglers calling it a night.

In all the time that I live with Ouma I never see her share her bed with anyone. I cannot remember whether there was ever a man in her life, except for Walter. His name rings out loud in her prayers. She beseeches her God with whys, in the silence of the night in the room that I share, with one window in the middle of two embossed wardrobes and a door that opens directly into the kitchen. It is there, half-asleep, where I listen, and see vivid images of two boys, Victor and Boetie, Walter's sons. They have been brought to KwaGuqa for Jwana to tend while their mother is in prison. Just like that, he appears after another of his long absences and drops them off for months or years or a long time. In addition to Uncle Bower and my mother, her two children, she now has an additional two sons, both straight-haired and blue-eyed, to raise. She does. When their mother is released from prison she comes to get them back. It is not Walter who comes. Ouma Mary stays for a week and she and Ouma Jwana strike up a sisterhood that outlasts the lives of Victor and Boetie. Ouma Mary has four more children and all of them are called Bowers and it irks Ouma, who wears her wedding ring like a sword. They remain a part of our family, always introduced to curious guests as my mother's brothers with the 'from another mother' murmured under the breath.

Before we move to Alexandra my uncles visit frequently, when they are not hindered by brief terms in prison for minor crimes like disturbing the peace and assault. The charges spiral with the degree of violence involved and the terms of imprisonment increase from weeks to months, past a year. Separately and within a small space of time, they die from the customary violence that is the emblem of broken countries. Straight from Doornfontein on Siemert Road, they give me wet, smelly kisses on the mouth when they come to visit their mama, my ouma. I wriggle with discomfiture, unaccustomed to effusive public shows of affection. Touching is a formality strictly observed for the arrivals and departures. My uncles are rough and no one messes with them as they are always ready to *donder* anyone who dares to call them *amperbaas* (almost boss). Ousie, they call my mother, and she is gentle and kind with them, no doubt recalling her own orphaning when she was a child and Ouma left her with Ouma Sussie to seek her fortune in Kimberley.

As a teenager, my mother must have understood their abject misery arriving in an African rural township at the house of their father's deserted African wife. It must have moved her. They do not speak isiNdebele and she is their mouthpiece in KwaGuqa. Jwana enfolds them into her home and they become her own and Mama starts her role as their foster mother. Victor and Boetie adore her, and of all my so-called coloured relatives, they are the only ones I remember as completely free of any show of racial discrimination. They love Ouma as if she were their own birth mother.

I know now that I was raised by a well-meaning woman, a passionate lover, maimed but unbowed by unrequited love or perhaps make-believe. I wonder if her fulsome prayers are also her way of telling me part of the story of her life. Or maybe she is just transported by the lonely silence, wrapped in the quiet of a woman alone in the company of a sleeping child and the flame of a candle. I lie still, waiting for her to speak to her God, alone, at ten o'clock at night. Lying in my bed with the lumpy coir mattress, pretending to be fast asleep. I wait. That is how I learn that Walter is a bounder who left her with two young children. My mother never ever speaks about her father to me. I never ask. What I hear from Ouma's bedtime prayers is at times overtaken by an overpowering drowsiness and when I wake up in the morning I have to look away from her naked face, afraid that I might see the traces of the silent tears fallen on her bosom.

✥ ✥ ✥

MY OUMA, like the Masekelas, is a committed member of the Lutheran Church. She makes regular contributions to the church fund and attends services every Sunday. I, on the other hand, attend the Anglican Church, where my mother was baptised and married. The ritual and formality of my church with its set prayers and responses is different from the direct and personal appeal of Jwana's church. She clings to her own church. I think it is also her choice that she raised my mother as Anglican. Even though Walter is an absent husband, Jwana insists that he is still the head of the household, ruling from the sepia photograph that hangs next to the marriage certificate and the wedding photograph of their unsmiling faces. Bearing his name granted her a certain respectability. She has not fallen. She is Mrs Johanna Bower, married to Walter 'by law'. This is one of the few phrases Ouma repeats for emphasis. She cannot speak English and since he is originally from Ladysmith, maybe they spoke to each other in isiZulu. *Ek is Walter se vrou* (I am Walter's wife) 'by law'! I suppose that, as children, my mother and her brother must have heard Ouma repeat this assertion many times, but I never asked my mother about this as I was always too bothered with my personal troubles, which would fade away as Ouma's grew and snapped me out of my mind.

My parents set up their new household in City Deep, away from Witbank. There in City Deep my father makes with his own hands a small garden with a rockery and a fishpond with water lilies. My father is a great gardener but in his fancy language he prefers to refer to his hobby as Landscape Design. So with the postage stamp garden of the City Deep cottage, which is the first home to which he brings his bride, he creates a wondrous garden for my mother. It is a showpiece in the small enclave of housing that has been created for the African clerical staff at the mine. Each little four-roomed house is fenced and has a neat little gate at the front with a tiny gardening space on either side of the path leading to the front door. This is the first time I have seen a rockery. There are a couple of small boulders with aloes and red-hot pokers massed between and in front of them, followed by smaller rocks and hundreds and hundreds of stones and pebbles, between which grow measured sizes of fat succulents, some rigidly armed with thorns. Best of all is the pond where the goldfish snake and dive, disappearing and reappearing between the canvas of round floating leaves of the waterlilies. On the other side of the path are cultivated flowering plants bordering the small square patch of green grass, where we sometimes sit on warm evenings.

It is the first of his seven gardens, some of which we visit periodically during our childhood. He leaves something, some artistic creation, wherever he lives.

Ouma's condition for my parents' marriage was that we, her grandchildren, were to be raised as Anglicans. In all the years for which we live in Witbank, Jwana and I go our separate ways to church as soon as we get to the corner of the street where the Lutheran church stands. Before she crosses the street, she watches me walk down the long main street past her enemy's house on the first corner and then on past George Mafuyana's butchery, at which point I wave to her and only then does she cross the street to her church. Bit by bit, as my responsibilities increase and I begin to help with more of the household tasks, I earn my place as her official reminder. My growing ability to read and to write, and to interpret the Witbank newspaper, grows me a place of importance and regard in the home we share. I anticipate her needs, understanding that, for instance, she is developing a headache because she needs a cup of tea. Or that I have to put the kettle on the stove as soon as Oupa Legoale settles himself on the armchair in the front room. People always need to have a fresh cup of tea and sometimes there are even some *soetkoekies* or Marie biscuits to serve with it.

I stitch together Uncle Bower's life from fragments I overhear about his temper and his anger. He was expelled from Kagiso Secondary School and broke Ouma's heart by refusing to continue his education. His only success seemed to have been on the football field. All of Witbank remembered him for his mastery of the game and, according to Hugh, he was the star of the Witbank Aces. As he scored goal after goal the spectators roared and shouted, 'Solomon Slow, son of a Scottish gentleman!' Ouma has never been to see him play but when Hugh dramatises his story she presses her lips together tightly, tilts back her head to hide her face as she raises her arms to fuss with her *doek* (headscarf). I do not ever remember my mother speaking of her father, but when I went to Ladysmith I found a big workman's house there with a tree in the backyard, which was the dwelling of a Walter Bower, registered at the Ladysmith Archive – which boasted one computer. In Dundee at the mine museum there was also a record of a Walter Bower who had come from Scotland with some infantry unit or other to defend the British colony.

Minkie, the firstborn son of the eldest living son, learns early to become a raconteur. When I fall ill after Khalo and Ouma's altercation, Ouma says that it is my illness that broke Minkie's quietness of speech. She says he told me wondrous stories that helped to stay the fever and the delirium. It was he who challenged the hovering angels of death at my bedside. I barely remember the details of that time, except when I smell the

smoke of incense or when I wake up in the middle of the night
dampened by an unexplained night sweat. Minkie, who is about
seven years old, is living in Payneville with Auntie Tinnie, Ouma
Sussie's last-born, Uncle Kenny, my father's youngest brother –
recently expelled from Kilnerton Training Institution – and my
parents. Our separation becomes the foundation of an unbroken
closeness, one which endures through the years when I continue
to live in KwaGuqa with Ouma, then when he goes to St Peter's
Secondary School when we move to Alexandra, then through my
five years at Inanda Girls' Seminary and his departure to London
in 1960 before I complete matric – through the twists
and turns of exile and return. It is what my father, in his self-
deprecating and bombastic turn of phrase, would have called 'all
the vicissitudes of life'.

Unlike my father, who is tall, dark and talkative, my Uncle
Bower is a short, strong man, softly spoken and quick in moving
his body, never rising up from a chair but shooting out with a
spectacular swoosh. He loves cracking his finger joints loudly or
pulling them out straight.

Khalo's motorbike is the bane of Ouma's life and when he
is out of her sight she imagines him in all grotesque shapes of
death wrought by this machine, which seduces him anew with
each burst of power. *Isithuthuthu*, it is aptly called in isiNdebele,
repeating the short bursts of noise coming from its engine. In-
tently, at the back of the yard near the shed for the wood and
coal, my uncle soaps it, rinses it, polishes it, buffs it, inspects it,
pats it and gives it one long sidelong look, almost tripping over
it as he reluctantly leaves it parked in the shade. He loves to race
his motorbike in the wind, in the sun, in the rain, when it is cold
and when it is hot, and in the disappearing light of dusk that
hangs briefly, competing with the smoke that snakes from the
chimneys all up and down the dusty streets. It is the only thing

that belonged to Walter Bower, the absent Scottish dandy from Ladysmith who was his father.

The boys, mostly our cousins and brothers, are not much older than me and my girl cousins, Wincie and Miriam, but already they know every corner of the location. They can roam free in groups, killing birds, trapping mice, stealing fruit from farms in the surrounding areas and sometimes swimming in toxic dams of mine water. They regularly go to watch football on the location football field and they also have special days for spying on local lovers in the veld.

Minkie, who knows every corner of KwaGuqa, is always ready to enact scenes of real and imagined events. His technicolour accounts are inspired by the films he has seen at the bioscope in Payneville. Overhearing these versions of overstated reality, my mother or Auntie Tinnie, when they are around, sometimes intervene and I am set free from my brother's marathon make-believe. They chide him with smiles as though it were the most natural thing for an elder brother to amuse his younger sister, but also tease me about believing everything I hear.

My recollection of Uncle Bower is patchy. What I still remember is that he would pick us up by lifting us up, off our feet, with both of his hands clasping our skulls and covering our ears. We smile through our gritted teeth going through this pain-ful exercise, which is mercifully brief. It earns us praise and the promise of a strong neck, but it is an ordeal even as we know we cannot refuse a gesture of affection from an adult. Older people always know best. Even though my mother never intervenes to stop the ritual, I know it fills her with disquiet as she waits to pull us back to the safety of her bosom afterwards. Uncle Bower promises us that this exercise is meant to make us grow tall. It was Walter's way with him.

My brother is not here any more and I cannot call him on the telephone to have all the details embellished or hear his plaintive *I am telling the truth, Babsie! That's what happened.*

Minkie can act out all Uncle Bower's moves, a sudden somersault, a swift toss of the ball on his heel, onto his head, then guiding it to the ground to kick for the spectacular goal that clanged through the kitchen window pane heading straight over the heads of my two grannies under the apricot tree, over the retaining wall, into the outside lavatory.

While I am awestruck by my brother's fantastical stories, it is the talk of my two grannies that I savour, the titbits I can pick up in between doing, fetching and taking for them.

But now I am sent to fetch Ouma Sussie and I will listen as they talk about Khalo's football match and coming home.

It is a moment taut with suspense, unknown outcomes wound around an emerging time fraught with its own threats. The one person who is my only companion is distracted. The one who never asks for help needs her sister. I will say to Ouma Sussie, she has received a letter, no matter how many questions she asks. I will not say the name Khalo.

Certainly, Khalo's father, my grandfather Walter Bower, is never featured in my grannies' reminiscences, just as Oupa Mtsweni, Ouma Sussie's husband, is a mystery. Everything on my maternal family's side points to the fact that men went away and came back to be buried. Both my granny sisters are widowed. For the first ten years of my life the only men who are constant are the select working men who come every early evening, eager to pass the evening repeating their woe-filled stories about their latest run-ins with their bosses at their workplaces.

I look forward to the arrival of the men. They break the monotony of the after-school chores and the sun-drenched silence occasionally ripped by a cock's crow, answered by a faraway bark of a lonely mongrel or the whistle of the goods train. Ticking to the slow rhythm of the passing minutes, childhood is a slow eternity, defying the promise of an approaching and unknown era forever looming in a new vocabulary of apartheid. We are surplus people, wandering in a landscape where at any time we can be ambushed by the uncertainty of edicts passed in a parliament we have not chosen. Boosted by the thirsty men, I, who can now read out confidently, await the moment when Uncle Basie asks me to read a chosen article in the newspaper aloud. In half-understanding, the words roll hesitantly from my thin lips, which Ouma says are like Walter's. But alas, my nose is of the Masekelas, as is the *kroes* (frizzy) hair that battles the comb and has to be tamed with four tight braids and a parting in the middle. The tangled hair and the broad nose. *Maar daardie onderlip is Walter s'n.* (But that bottom lip is Walter's.) I hate it that parts of myself belong to other people, even dead ones I do not know, like Walter.

In that newspaper, removals, strikes, natives, *swart gevaar*, Bantu Education, passes, arrests, imprisonment, found guilty, executed and, in between, always police this and that.

I hate the thunderstruck silence of rainy days when lightning flashes and the rain drums loudly on our zinc roof. But later, in the dark of the night when I search for the pot under the bed, the soft rhythm of a gentle rain pattering on the roof is like a lullaby to sink me deeper into a sweet slumber punctuated by Ouma's rhythmic snoring.

A clap of lightning, unexpected and blinding bright, signals a rush to cover mirrors and windows with old newspapers and cloth. In this way, it is believed, we can direct the white fire away from ourselves. God speaks His power through the weather and now apartheid is also thrown into the mix of things to fear. There are dangers everywhere, and after the storm the stories the men tell are enlivened by anecdotes of the many ways in which lightning can kill.

One cold winter morning, my sister Elaine runs from the kitchen window, shouting in isiNdebele, 'The sky is raining powdered soap, Ouma!' Indeed, white powder is falling silently from the skies. It is snow. We are to stay indoors, Jwana declares, until it passes.

That night the topic for the men is snow and they tell fantastical tales of how it can weigh down a grown man until he falls to the ground and dies. But then there is always something new to know and the origins of the tales are always hearsay. The whispers, for instance, about putting a needle on the railroad track to derail the steam engine that rumbles the goods trains past the location every day. Or that if you examine the eyes of deceased subjects in photographs their pupils are dulled, unlike those of living people. More interestingly, you are not supposed to wash spectacles because soap and water interfere with the medicine inside the glass, causing malfunction. (I see my mother hide her mild amusement when I tell her this one. She stresses the importance of cleanliness and how it makes for clarity to have clean glasses.)

In the daytime the streets are empty and the groups of schoolchildren trickle down and I am alone by the time I turn into Tollman Street, which is almost at the end of KwaGuqa. Ouma is leaning on the wall of the veranda, looking out for me.

My father and uncles are visitors and they sit in the front room. The conversation of the men who come to drink is strictly monitored and it is stipulated that they cannot raise their voices or swear. When Minkie comes to stay during school holidays when I am seven I beat him at several games of draughts. He is also trounced in a few games by the men and they declare I am a champion. Ouma intervenes decisively. Minkie will not be playing any more. He does not need to mist his brain with draughts, she declares, because his piano lessons are more important. His mind needs rest to make way for the school lessons, which are more important for his education. My bubble bursts.

In the low conversation around the big table in the middle of the kitchen, away from the benches lined up against the wall, the men talk about the *khalabayi*. The colour bar is a toxic agency that permeates every aspect of the very air we breathe; it cuts through the cheer and glooms the air so that the men drink deeper. It is the reason for everything, and when I am a child it is the explanation for everything that had to do with everyone I knew. It is the reason why people disappear, die, get sick, lose their houses and their lives. Even the weather has a colour bar, because lightning seems to stalk Africans sheltering under a tree in a thunderstorm and tornados level shanty towns where Africans live. Only black people get arrested for not having passes, people are removed from farms because of their colour, people and children die from diseases because of the colour bar. It is, ultimately, the reason why Uncle Bower too would be its victim, as were the men who drowned on the *Mendi*. When I think of the *Mendi*, I start to paint pictures of men screaming and running in the dark, throwing themselves into the water and being swallowed up, disappearing into the cold sea.

My grannies sometimes speak of their Mabena male relatives and recall stories of how they were removed from the farms where they were born and raised. And how they are scattered in places like Bronkhorstspruit, Ogies, Minnaar and Welgedacht. These are *dorpies* where the train stops on the way to the bigger towns like Springs, Boksburg and Brakpan before it reaches the city of Johannesburg where, in my infant understanding, grown men are sometimes swallowed up by the mine dumps and never seen again. The old women sigh and say of a prodigal son or a philandering husband, *Wadliwa izindunduma!* (Swallowed by the mine dumps!) Danger seems to lurk everywhere, not least in the picture of Walter in the front room. I frighten myself replaying the stories I have overhead so that I dread the eyes of my grandfather, whose stern mien guards the guest bedroom from which there is always something I have to fetch. The recollections are layered and it is only much later, when I can no longer ask Ouma about them, that I remember the different versions of the same story. As for other men close to the Mabena family, they are itinerant labourers scattered on the Boer farms dotted across the Eastern Transvaal.

There is also mention of the war and bitter complaint about how the returning African soldiers were duped. And there is the madman who strolls the streets with a permanent wariness, looking suspiciously at everything around him. He is haunted by commanding voices, which tell him to march in time. Away from the eyes of the elders, some of the boys run to keep up with him, exaggerating his limp. They chortle in amusement as they compete to mimic him. At any moment he turns around in fury, shooting an imaginary rifle, scattering the mock troops in every direction. Or his face just crumples and he sits down and sobs loudly, cupping his ears with his hands, his long slender fingers trembling in time with his shaking body. He, too, lives with his old grandmother and Ouma shakes her head sadly, intoning, '*Arme skepsel* (Poor creature), he was such a fine young man before he went to the white people's *oorlog* (war).' I learn then that there have been many wars, some in our own country and others in faraway countries where there is snow, and only white soldiers are allowed to carry arms.

But my grandfather Walter Bower was never a soldier. He was a tall, moustachioed figure posing stiffly in the wooden-framed sepia photograph alongside the wedding certificate. He took her all the way to the Johannesburg Magistrate's Court to make a decent woman of her. Later, when I become intoxicated with the written word, I wonder how they managed their conversations since her English words are few and 'dammit' is her most favourite. Like most people of her age, her dog-eared Hollandse Bijbel is her proof of scholarship.

The new Afrikaans, then being developed as an official language by the Nationalist government that comes to power when I am seven years old, she despises and calls a new-fangled thing. Something, she says, that is made up and impure, designed for the petty officials to impose their evil *khalabayi* on *swart mense* (black people), something that makes new laws that are meant to confuse and cause disarray. But then she shifts her mood to extol the genius of white men who could make flying machines. 'Yes, they are clever people. The only thing they cannot do, have never succeeded in doing, is to create a living being.'

I can never understand where Walter Bower features in all this musing and I do not dare to disturb these rare, free-flowing outbursts that are in great contrast to her reticence about things personal to her. Soon afterwards, she begins humming her nameless songs and I offer to make her a cup of tea. '*Dankie, my meisiekind*,' she says, with a faraway look in her eyes. Looking back, now, I realise that this is a stage in her life when I begin to become her friend.

As I reflect on my early life, and when I think that I returned to South Africa in 1990 at the age of forty-nine, after twenty-seven years in exile, and then proceeded with a working life until I was almost seventy, I am filled with awe and anger that Ouma was only in her fifties when she started raising Minkie and me. I shudder to think of all the South African oumas whose mangled lives have been concealed by events so scathing that all that remains is to eke out some joy in having survived. They have soldiered many kinds of wars so that they can now raise their own grandchildren. What they have seen from a blighted childhood and accelerated maturation drones in their minds, choking the words to explain the journeys they have been forced to take, so they hum away, forever burying the past that relentlessly rears its head with the mask of the *khalabayi* now resurrected as apartheid.

✧ ✧ ✧

ONE OF the pastimes of the older boys is to scout the veld beyond the railway line, past the wrecked grassland and the man-made holes where the blanketed four-gallon tins are buried at nightfall to ferment underground. Below these manholes are the mines, and further along is the goods train railway line, the boundary with the white farms ahead, just past the bush that fully separates them from the Native Location, where we live in neat wire-fenced plots, back to back and side by side, with the only entrances on the street. There is no hiding from your neighbours.

The boys scour the veld, disturbing the trysts of couples in the bush. Unsuspecting, the victims perform their exuberant acts with speed and greed, at ease that only the blue sky is a witness. Later on the boys mimic them in gross groans and cries, grunting and sighing and then bursting into laughter. It separates the boys from the girls. For us girls, their actions foster unease and shame.

Uncle Bower never lives with us in the house. He occupies one of the rooms in the backyard next to Uncle Basie's, who rents the other room in our backyard.

Ouma is always up at dawn, to start her day but also in part to ensure that no illicit activities that would fail to pass her muster occurred after lock-up at nine o'clock.

Already notorious for sleeping through the loudest and merriest events, one morning I am woken by shouts in the backyard. Jumping out of bed in fright I see Ouma dragging Mira's daughter towards the back gate and Uncle Bower with a ripped and bloody shirt, unable to match her strength and ferocity, struggling to stop her. Tilly is her name. I am crying and Minkie runs to Ouma Sussie's house for help. By the time Uncle Putu, Auntie Tinnie and Ouma Sussie come, Ouma's thumb is hanging loosely from her hand and she is hoarse with fury, shouting 'Out, out of my house, whore!'

Ouma insists that the police be called and my bleeding Uncle Bower, now black-eyed, is taken away, thrown screaming into the back of the police van. By then he is babbling incoherently and in court he will not speak out. He is committed to a mental hospital.

It is a family legend that I became critically ill after the fight and that for months I lay in bed in delirium and fever and that even the white doctor in Witbank could not diagnose my illness. Minkie swears that he sat by my bedside and held my hand, telling me stories as the adults prayed for me to get well.

The anger that Ouma feels towards Mira starts long before Minkie and I are born. All I know is that Walter Bower was involved. On his rare visits to KwaGuqa he spent far too much time at Mira's place, fraternising with merrymakers. Tilly's crime was that she was Mira's daughter and nothing could endear her to Ouma. Neither Tilly nor Uncle Bower knew why. There was an untold secret: something had happened, of which no one dared speak. It had to do with that time when Mira's house was the toast of KwaGuqa. Tilly and Uncle Bower's liaison should never have been. According to Ouma, they had lured my uncle into their house of sin and used Tilly to enslave him in body and in mind, just as they had done with Walter. All this was designed to destroy her and her whole family.

Ouma's hatred, already deep, is sealed when Minkie, visiting from Springs for the school holidays, is run over by Mira's son on his motorbike. They vow it was an accident, but my granny swears it was a calculated act. So does Minkie. My brother, then about ten years old, bleeding and bruised, is confirmation of the Miras' aim to destroy us, one by one, starting with the males. We are not privy to the beginnings of the hostilities but by virtue of blood ties we are instructed to take our places on the side of the just, led by Ouma.

Sometimes I overhear disconnected recollections of the early days from my two grannies. The accident is a sequel to the war about Tilly and Uncle Bower's subsequent departure for good. Minkie has a scar to show for it for all of his life, just above one of his eyes; to the end, like Ouma, he swears that it was a deliberate act of malice. As I remain all my life, the younger sister, I also begin to learn how to hold on to my own truths but at the same time give the appearance of opting out of arguments. Keeping the peace and moving on allows me the space to thrive on my own imaginings.

As for the Miras, we were not to speak with them or take anything from them, and we were to report any sighting of them, no matter how remote, to Ouma in detail. Although all older people have titles to their names, like Sisi, Boetie, Auntie, Uncle, Oupa, Ouma, and so on, the Miras were so low in Ouma's esteem that we were allowed to call them by name.

At one point, Mira is so poor that he goes begging for a drink or a piece of bread – to keep body and soul together, as my father would have said. I remember Ouma chasing him away like a dog once, when he came to beg for food: '*Voetsek, hond!*' (Get lost, dog!) I hear her say to him, using the very words she had forbidden me to use. He is living in his dilapidated old house with phantoms no one else can see. Sometimes when we pass by his house we hear him pleading, *No, no, no.* They say it is because he is drinking too much liquor, but I hear Ouma say it is the ghosts of all the people he has killed who are now haunting him. He is old and frail and I pity him. Mama says he has something called pellagra. But in the language of the street he is suffering from the *horris* (horrors). He has frightening visions that cause him to cover his eyes and his ears.

✤ ✤ ✤

TELEGRAMS HAVE always been the bane of Ouma's life. Designed to transmit urgent critical information, they are the standard way of reporting death in the wars of life. Since – unlike whites – we have no telephones, the delivery of the dreaded yellowish envelope means someone close is dead. Killed at work in the mine, at the factory or on the streets of a native location far away on the Gold Reef. It is the deaths of farmworkers that take months or more before they are reported from the dry lips of men and women who whisper and glance over their shoulders when recounting the death, as if fearing the murderers would overhear them and pounce.

Ouma complains bitterly about how casually my parents send telegrams to announce their visits. She thought telegrams were only meant to announce deaths. But soon after the letter incident when I was ordered to fetch Ouma Sussie, another telegram arrives.

'Read it to me, Babsie. There is a foreboding in my heart.' She hands it to me.

ARRIVING WITH TEAM FOR SUNDAY FOOTBALL MATCH.
COMING HOME AFTER GAME.

'Read it again!' I watch as my ouma's frown bursts into a big smile. Tears falling, she whispers, '*My Almagtige Here.*' (My Almighty God.)

The biggest challenge of the ensuing weeks is to keep Khalo's visit a secret, especially from Mira. Although he is now demented and harmless, Ouma abhors him still, with a passion, and does not put it past him to harm Khalo.

On the appointed day, when the pots are cooked and the front table laid with the dinner set and the glasses that never see the light otherwise, we wait and wait.

The rose bush is heavy with buds and some of the flowers are already blooming. I count them carefully. There are exactly nine of them. I do not like it, the odd number; it does not bode well for Ouma and me.

Maybe it means he will not come to us. The pansies are blooming, their small faces reaching out to the sun in purple, velvet-orange – all the colours of the rainbow. The light breeze causes them to nod their little heads. The hollyhocks are weighed down with blooms, their slender stems bending down from the neck in pink and blue, red and white, apricot and deep berry colours, and then suddenly something rests on my neck. I plunge my hand into the hollow between the two sharp bones in the middle of my chest and catch the little creature.

It is a ladybird, the lucky omen, the great messenger in Ndebele culture. Tenderly, I examine her to see if she has been hurt. Her wings point in the direction of the football field as she tries to escape. She is beautiful, a dark rust colour with bold black spots.

I whisper to her: '*Poli poli*, tell me true. Is he coming today? *Poli poli*, if you give me one little hint about the day, I will let you fly away. *Poli poli*, it is my grandmother I want to see happy. Please take a message to him. Tell him we love him dearly. *Poli poli*, tell him all will be forgiven if he comes home.'

I whisper gently to *poli poli* and she stops struggling and sits quietly in my hand. I choose the most beautiful pansy for her and place her in its soft petals. Soon she stretches out her wings and flies away.

I turn the corner of the house and peep into the kitchen and the most delicious smells smack me in the face. The meal is obviously for a great number of people. There are chickens in the oven, beef stew with dumplings simmering on the stove, and an array of smaller pots at the side of the stove with rice, pumpkin, sweet potatoes, green beans and all the favourite foods for special occasions. I cannot think of anything to say.

Then we hear the noise of the crowd. 'Solomon Slow, son of a Scottish gentleman!' They are screaming. His team has won the game and he has scored two of the winning goals. At the corner they turn right into Tollman Street and we see my uncle above the crowd, carried by his singing teammates. All of four feet and nine inches, Johanna stands at the front door to receive her only son. Wordless, at last they embrace.

But it is not for long. They have to return to Brakpan that night. He says it will only be for a while. He just has to wind up his affairs. He will be back. She need not worry any more.

I have never seen so many people in our house, in the yard at the back; some of the locals are just hanging about on the street.

It is hardly a month later when another telegram comes. Confident that it is announcing Khalo's arrival date, Ouma hands it to me to read.

SOLOMON BOWER DEAD. CONTACT POLICE BRAKPAN.

He played another match, this time in Boksburg. After the match, riding home with his mates, all on their bicycles and he on his motorbike, they noticed a bakkie full of young white men, which seemed to be following them. There was something ominous in the gestures of the men in the motor vehicle. They were telling them to stop. Quickly the cyclists conferred, their voices muffled by the blowing wind. Some would run into the bush where the van could not follow, others would swerve back in the opposite direction. Khalo demurred. He would be able to speed away and elude them, he must have thought. But they caught up with him and threw him into the back of the open van. They drove into one of the plantations off the road to an open clearing they had already prepared.

It is here that his body is found. Left for dead.

Over and over, my ouma tells the story of his last hours, which she pieces together from the evidence she gleans from some of his mates and what she has seen with her own eyes. For weeks I listen to the questions that will remain unanswered, and the small details of her own making.

Why didn't his friends report the matter to the police immediately?

Then again, would the police have responded with urgency to a black man's death?

What did it matter that a black man had been abducted by white men on a lonely road?

Was it possible that one of his team mates, the one who suggested they abandon their bikes, was involved in the plot to murder Khalo?

Why did Khalo not leave his bike and run into the bush with his friends?

Yes, his white handkerchief was full of clotted blood. He had tried to blow his nose before he died.

There were marks on the ground that showed that he had moved when he regained consciousness. Moving to get home, perhaps thinking of his promise to return to his mother. His nails were full of the red soil, showing how he had crawled, ignoring his pain, pushing to get home. His teeth, his eyes, his head, the bruises on his body – she could remember every welt, every kick of the boot and all the fists put together. Listening as a child to what white men can do, I am afraid. It never occurred to me that she already knew all of this as a child growing up in the latter part of the nineteenth century near Middelburg, just like her parents and their parents, for ever and ever, amen.

The soil under his nails as he awakened from unconsciousness and tried to scratch his way out of the darkness.

Only one shoe returned to her, with bloodied clothes.

Years later, when my Auntie Tinnie is almost eighty years old, I think she can tell me more about Khalo.

'No, I can't remember anything but the smell of his body in the house, on the way to the cemetery, until we covered his box with soil. It smelled. That is all I remember, the stench.'

That is what Auntie Tinnie says and I am angry with her for forgetting. I think, *That is what she wants to remember*, and that it is unfair to Uncle Bower. But to this day I have a strong sense of smell and I love green perfume.

OUMA REFUSES to attend the trial in Brakpan. It will not bring him back, she says. Two Afrikaner youths are tried for his death. They worked in the same butchery with him. He had several altercations with them, refusing to call them *baas*. They receive a suspended sentence of three months in jail for culpable homicide and a fine of one hundred pounds.

Soon thereafter, in 1952, we move to Alexandra to live with my parents.

THREE

ALEXANDRA

I WENT to Inanda Seminary, a girls' school, at the age of fourteen in 1956, still weighed down by my experience as a coloured at City and Suburban Coloured School in the inner city of Johannesburg.

At my previous school, St Michael's Anglican School in Alexandra, the principal was Mr Obed Phahle, and he and his wife were family friends; besides, my father was the Chief Health Inspector of Alexandra and I was known as *ngoana wa spektere* (the inspector's child). My best friend was Msuthukazi Mbere, and both of her brothers, Aggrey and Jiyane, were my brother's best friends.

At City and Suburban I was nobody and nearly nothing. In Alex, with a population of about eighty thousand, most responsible citizens knew one another, as was usually the case in the older urban townships on the Reef. In particular, it was the professional class – nurses, doctors, teachers, religious leaders, businessmen and politicians – who were respected for the work they did out in the township. Mostly they are known by their surnames with the prefix of their profession. This is also the unlettered person's way of paying homage to the power of educational achievement, which was in direct contrast to the disrespectful and humiliating behaviour of the apartheid officials towards pillars of township society. Many of these officials were new to the big city, the ridges of their rubber soles still patched with dried mud from last year's rains. They could not abide the manners or the style of 'city blacks', who did not know their place, who could earn more money than them, and who lived in better houses and in neighbourhoods too close to the public housing provided for poor whites, like themselves, who had barely completed high school.

Now, with the new apartheid laws, blacks would no longer hold skilled jobs by law. In the factories, the mines, the railways and all public works, the apartheid officials held the reins and, irrespective of how well Africans were educated, they would always work under white supervision. The apartheid officials were not used to being in the proximity of so many educated blacks, some of whom had the cheek to respond in English only. In the small towns they came from, no kaffir was out on the streets after sunset; night time in the streets was for Europeans only. They had what my mother likes to call 'a complex', which compelled them to carry out gratuitous acts of physical and mental violence towards blacks.

But it was the criminal element, who were called tsotsis – mostly victims of poverty and unemployment, or genuine psychotic victims of the racist system – who also wrought mayhem on the lives of their fellow blacks, to the delight of the security forces, who regularly arrived at the scene of the crime long after the event. In addition to preying on the poor and robbing them of their hard-earned cash, abducting women and raping them was commonplace. African women had always been at the bottom of the totem pole, just as they still were when I was entering early womanhood. They absorbed the bias of patriarchy at home, at the workplace and in society in general, not least from the tsotsis, who also had a particular dislike for what they

called 'situations', a tag they used for the educated middle class –
presumably because this class loved the use of long English words.

They could carry out their black-on-black violence with
ease because the police only pounced when the crime impinged
on the white community. In Alexandra I shared the perils and
fighting spirit of survival with everyone, all was in the open.
At my Coloured School the air was decisively that of detach-
ment, no connection with a particular community or sense of
belonging. I disappeared into myself, maintaining a cool exterior
that belied the churning emotions that sometimes had me
running back and forth to the girls' lavatories. My heart raced
with fear that I would lose control, or act rashly in reaction to
the invisibility that had been thrust upon me. Ouma had not
prepared me for this!

Sometimes, when things were not going well, I would remind
myself of how my mother had also had bad times. She never
spoke of those events and I only knew about them because Ouma
told me. It was our secret. She had come back from Kimberley
after an absence of almost a year. This was not uncommon in the
African locations. Many young women left their children with
relatives to go and find employment in the towns and cities where
mining and early industrialisation had resulted in pockets of
residential areas notorious for their squalor, crime and, from the
point of view of whites, their multiracialism. Unlike the other
women, Johanna had a prodigal husband, who was white and,
at the time, one of the 'adventurers' in Kimberley. I suspect he
called for Johanna because he was in genuine need of a 'partner'
in some of his 'business' activities.

She once told me of how some sold polished glass in the
place of real diamonds. They displayed the 'diamonds' in a flash
and the exchange of money was just as quick, and then they
disappeared into the night, never to be seen in those parts again.

This unexpected candour was soon retracted by a swift closure of the topic and the announcement of a sudden errand to be run. But it was Walter who had made it possible for her to return to KwaGuqa with a pouch full of money to build the house I called home.

✤ ✤ ✤

IT WAS soon after Ouma and I had left KwaGuqa to live in Alexandra that my father brought a present for Mama. It lay around, on the kitchen table, in the bag with her knitting and once even under the wooden cover of her Singer sewing machine. It was a book called *God's Stepchildren* by Sarah Gertrude Millin. She peered at the cover suspiciously and put it back into the brown paper bag. She was knitting an elaborate cable-knit jersey from a pattern in *Woman's Weekly* and was caught up in counting stitches, picking up and casting off and observing the emerging pattern impatiently. She seemed unable to sustain her interest in the book, which she read in fits and starts, and once I heard her speak to it under her breath: 'Nonsense! Rubbish! Oh no!'

She was alone in the kitchen and it scared me to hear her speak so sharply to no one in the room. I was haunted by the insanity of Uncle Bower and the stories of mad men at the hospital when people would come back from visiting him. When I caught my mother in deep thought, it scared me that her eyes were unmoving and her body was still, listening to her own heartbeat. I could not leap over the precipice to her side. It reminded me of Uncle Bower and I would fear that she would also fly away.

My father's silences were always comfortable. In between he would say something about the grain of the table's wood or ask you to find his cigarettes and matches. Even when he was studying for one of the many health inspection exams he was always taking, he would share some newly discovered minutiae about a poison or a bacterium that fascinated him. He did not expect you to memorise these details, but he just could not resist sharing them with you. Otherwise he was the one to smash silences, often with unconsidered words that were not meant to cut but nevertheless left a mark. Such was the occasion when he came home one evening and found the book he had given my mother open on the table. I don't remember his exact words but he was light-hearted, meaning no harm and, in his usual fashion, chuckling to himself before delivering his big English word for the day: 'My dear, what's the latest on miscegenation?'

My mother glared at him, her eyes just brimming with tears, then in a single movement she swept the book across the table towards him. It was unlike her to show her temper and the nearest I saw her come to an act of violence – except once, when she pinched me on the insides of my thighs because I had let the meat burn. My parents each raised a hand to me once and the humiliation of that violence has stuck with me, yet I have forgotten the pain of the cane on the bare palm, which was the bane of primary school. All I understand is that it separated me from each of them in a manner that living apart from them never did. They were still father and mother but they became man and woman, pedestrian, something less than I had ever imagined. They broke a promise – one that they had never made, but that I was entitled to trust they would keep. We were not a touching family. We did not hug, kiss. By touching me in anger they had gone beyond the boundary I did not even know was in place.

We did not know many so-called coloureds, except my mother's relatives in Doornfontein. They were distinguished by the fact that they did not speak any African language and had no interest in learning one. But there were people who lived in the African townships who looked like my mother and, unlike her, spoke neither English nor Afrikaans. There were no special houses or schools for them. No one remarked on their hair or the colour of their eyes. Like my great-grandmother, Ouma Kappie, their hair was not a crown of superiority; they stuffed it away under a *doek*. In short, it was not remarkable to be of mixed blood. Having found yourself in a particular community, you did all the customary activities as and when they were done in your community. Generally, if you were not white you went to a black school, and you spoke whatever language was common where you lived, and sometimes there were several. Even when your surname was Tollman or Smith, you slaughtered to respect the ancestors. Prior to the apartheid era, people seemed to navigate across the mixed-race issue sans the self-conscious deliberation that marks race relations today. The ruthless and accelerated programmes designed to entrench white racial superiority seem to have strengthened the social imperatives of *ubuntu* within the beleaguered African community, which, in turn, became even more inclusive and embracing, especially of those born within their society, irrespective of their genetic background. It was officialdom that proliferated the use of ethnic terms like 'coloured'. African custom bound all human beings together precisely because they differed from animals in their behaviour. Of course, there were exceptions to this rule, and some individuals, even among the oppressed, succumbed to a bigotry that was characterised by the use of pejorative terms to demean and belittle those who were deemed different in their appearance.

Even a cursory look at the events that occurred in the Eastern Transvaal from the arrival of the Voortrekkers until the conquest of the Ndebele and Pedi kingdoms reveals that a veritable assemblage of nationalities were involved in the mixed bag of incursions, raids, ambushes, battles and hunts that took place between the settlers and the indigenous groups. A photograph taken during the Boer War of the legendary Steinaecker's Horse, a volunteer military unit fighting for the British, is particularly instructive, showing the captured mercenaries of all racial colours with their local women and children. Significantly, several of the white men hold children of mixed race on their knees.

It was not the indigenous South Africans who invented the term 'coloured'. In historical time and with increasingly segregated residential areas, certain words like 'Hottentot', 'Boesman' and even 'Griqua' began to develop into pejorative terms, denoting inferiority and the contempt of the speaker towards the referent. The indigenous groups became the 'other' of the Europeans, and distinct from the Africans, whose languages often did not gain recognition until the missionaries installed themselves as proxies between the settlers and the new converts. In the urban areas, the speakers of these new African languages morphed into a buffer between the settlers and the indigenous people. So, it seems that, from the earliest times in South Africa, the term 'coloured' had to do with how one was perceived by the 'superior' white Europeans. As there were many people of mixed race who lived within the black community as blacks, it is clear that the mixed-race individual would choose a side, especially as that side became identified with certain privileges that were not enjoyed by Africans. It was a self-identification that was freely chosen, a decision to separate oneself, a breakaway into the void of the in-between into which others had thrust one. The first people of South Africa were only acknowledged on the new coat of arms in 1994. Hitherto, as the textbooks claimed, they had become extinct through wars, disease and their love of the European 'spirits', which they drank of so deeply because they liked to be drunk, to sing and to dance when they were not stealing or fighting; most so-called coloureds chose to follow their line of descent to Europe, eschewing their African side.

What is remarkable about the coloured identity is its elusiveness. At the very moment when you characterise it in a particular way, colouredness sprouts another meaning, which can be a contradiction or another layer of complexity that smacks you hard in the face for your presumptuousness or short-sightedness. Sometimes it is how you look that determines how you act, and sometimes it is the other way around. It trumps place of origin, colour of skin, nature of hair and other physical traits. Each of these attempts at definition are untrue in practice because they are all generalisations that do not admit exceptions. A colouredism or colouredness is a delicate, if not downright offensive, subject and no amount of discretion can rid it of sexuality, which clings like dried glue on the dark skin of the female – who is usually the ultimate victim as she gives issue to the mixed-race child. The white father bears no prejudice or moral condemnation, especially in the patriarchal context of our society. Colouredism is an unhealthy concept that divides, alienates and estranges. In our country, over the centuries, it has permeated every aspect of our culture and it is a virulence that begins and ends with the ignorance that keeps you imprisoned in an English or Afrikaans bubble, divorced from the political reality of white supremacy, of which we are all victims.

Don't go looking for coloureds in African countries. They exist only in the damaged minds of those coming out of a racist society like South Africa. They are extinct in the Caribbean, as Bob Marley has sung to you, just as George Lamming, Jamaica Kincaid and Langston Hughes have written to us. At one of the many stages of racism in the United States they went as far as classifying people according to the estimated amount of 'white blood' they had. So, one dictionary has sixty-two synonyms for people whose parents come from different races. When it was not enough to say mulatto, they spoke of octoroons and quadroons and even sank to the level of describing folk with the same words usually used to indicate the pedigree of animals.

But here I was, thirteen years old, faking the truth about who I really was, denying my father because of Bantu Education.

My mother's argument for registering me at the Coloured School, before Inanda, was a calculated one. Throughout that year it was trotted out to anyone who had questions about it. None could argue with her view that the Bantu Education Act was a travesty, unabashedly designed to halt the progress of African children so that they would not be able to compete except within the narrow confines of the Bantustans. Worse still, the emphasis of Bantu Education was on menial tasks performed in service of the white minority; it was regressive, utilising the most conservative aspects of African culture and tradition at a time when the colonised in Africa and beyond were making a leap into self-determination in a modern world they had helped to make possible. Especially in the two world wars.

The decision to send me to the Coloured School had been deliberately arrived at so that I could escape Bantu Education. I would be able to write matric a year earlier, since coloureds only spent two years doing their Junior Certificate. Having done my matric a year earlier, I would be in time to enter an open university like Wits, just before the so-called Extension of University Education Act became law. Mama was unapologetic about her derision for the narrowly ethnic universities that were mushrooming all over the country under the guise of development along 'own lines'. And she was not alone in that ferocious attitude. Many of my parents' friends and relatives who worked in the system abhorred Bantu Education and all the other trappings of apartheid policy. In the political field we know the names of the great freedom fighters, the ones who were prepared to die.

But in every province and every town and city there were men and women teachers who took up a public position to oppose Bantu Education. They were dismissed, banned from teaching anywhere in the country and imprisoned.

I walked from Noord Street to Polly Street in time for the 8:30 am opening bell and then at 2:30 pm I walked to Noord Street to catch the bus to Alex before the rush hour. My father had taken me on the bus and on a practice walk to the school before the term started. He had also wanted to show me the Polly Street Art Centre, which he frequented, to see the work of African artists. At the time the art training centre was headed by Cecil Skotnes, the exceptional South African artist whose own work was greatly influenced by that of his African students.

I maintained a calm exterior but inside I was seething throughout that year at City and Suburban. Despite the fact that I excelled in my schoolwork, no one seemed too keen to befriend me. I had nothing to offer with my kinky, non-European hair and yellowish complexion with no rose in it. I was ignored and unnoticed despite my outstanding performance in class. The girls swarmed around their straight-haired peers with pony tails and long plaits hanging down their backs. The most important moment of each day was when I would collect my books and leave the school premises.

At home I would be prickly and stingy about the details of my day. I did not have the words to describe my feelings without sounding self-centred, something my mother despised. I could not describe the subtle gestures of exclusion I had felt. I did not know how to say that the other girls made me feel ugly or that they had no curiosity about who I was, even though that would have interfered with my impostor role. It was what I later learnt: the silent treatment is a form of subtle exclusion that cannot be proved. Teachers ignored my raised hand because my answers were always right. And to my own shame I never spoke to the African workers on the school grounds. And I over-head some saying 'kaffir' and I did not immediately *donder* them. It was much, much more, but the words evaded me. It was the precision and the speed. A fleeting movement of the eye here, an incomplete signal there, all in the shrug of the shoulder before turning away.

With the plan that had been agreed between my parents there was no problem, but as the story spread the matter of my changed surname, from Masekela to Maskell for the Coloured School, became the crux. The highlight was the rape of my father's male authority.

Soon the story spread among our extended family and their friends. The matter of my surname became the crux of the whole matter, and it began to grow tentacles, each with a tighter grip. It went against male authority, a sacrosanct value in our patriarchal national life. As the murmurs grew, my father became less certain about the wisdom of his original approval. But Mama was un-apologetic about my registration at the school. She also defended Hugh's growing interest in music, standing up for his right to develop the talent of his choice.

Ouma had left to go and live in her new house in Enner-dale and my sisters Elaine and Sybil were with her. My parents were now arguing about my father's intention to get a job in Natalspruit, Germiston. We were to leave Alexandra, to live in another house supplied by his employers, but Katlehong was a typical apartheid-era location with carefully laid-out ethnic areas. In fact, there was a Mr Buitendacht who was a superintendent there. They knew him from the early days when he had been a clerk in Payneville, but he was now the big boss of Natalspruit.

My mother had a strong sense that our lives were regressing and she was very unhappy that she could not get a job with the

Johannesburg Welfare Department. In the midst of all this, my main worry was how I was going to explain the spelling of my name on the report submitted to Inanda. When I look back on the breakup of my family, I understand sharply the anger of my mother and that everything after her inability to be part of the Defiance Campaign just became a cover-up for her anger. She had been fired up by the Defiance Campaign. It was not a passing fancy. Both my parents worked among the poor, who were at the coalface of the injustice of the influx control laws, where a stamp on a document could uproot you and fling you into the unknown. The surprise arrival of my father's cousins to 'persuade' her and 'reason' with her to abandon her political activities was something she never forgave.

My mother, only five feet tall, was at the height of her beauty, and she coupled her brilliant career as a social worker with political activism by joining the ANC as a member during the period when the organisation was seized with drawing up plans for the Defiance Campaign. Her plans to go forward and be a volunteer for the Defiance Campaign were thwarted. A delegation of prominent dignitaries from my father's Batlokwa clan swooped unexpectedly into our house one Saturday evening as my mother was preparing dinner. They had been invited by my father. She was called in after I had served the tea and homemade scones, which we saved in the round tins elaborately decorated with idyllic European scenes of young mothers with their angelic offspring frolicking in the woods. She walked in like a warrior and, about three hours later, came out shrunken and wrung out. She had been counselled, harangued, warned and commanded in no uncertain terms that no Masekela woman would ever become a freedom fighter. Finish and *klaar*, as the saying goes.

I had shared in her excitement about the Defiance Campaign. At the square a street away from our house, I had – with other children, on the fringes of the meetings – heard many speeches made by the likes of Sisulu, Mandela, Kotane and other firebrands of the ANC. *Mayibuye iAfrika* echoed all over Alexandra, which was now also under the threat of forced removals. I sympathised with my mother. Deep down, I must have resolved to uphold her cause as soon as I became an adult woman. But I definitely resolved that no man would decide the path of my life.

The 1950s heralded a prominent role for African women in politics. It was a seminal era in the organisational power of women's politics. Women like Lillian Ngoyi, Helen Joseph, Frances Baard, Florence Matomela and many more matched foot to foot the abilities of their male counterparts in the movement. In part, the unexpected militance of rural women in Zeerust, Cato Manor and many other hamlets had given men in the apartheid government and in the ANC pause. The women had shown their mettle in organising highly successful campaigns, culminating in the 1956 Women's March to the Union Buildings. The majority of the women were from the urbanised working class, at the sharp end of the apartheid knife of joblessness, influx control and the countless regulations that spelt indignity, suffering and humiliation. Despite the severe sentences, fines and imprisonment, the women persisted in resistance. Photographs of women beating men out of beerhalls, being chased by baton-wielding policemen and being sjambokked and herded into *kwela-kwelas* (police vans) were frequently splashed across the front pages of *Drum, Zonk!* and the *Golden City Post* – as were those of women who had been dumped with their household goods in the empty veld of the Bantustans.

Being removed from the historical protests of her era came at great cost to Mama. On one level, she never forgave my father, but on another level she had made the choice to put family first. It was the beginning of the end of their marriage.

She had compromised her principles to save her marriage and keep her family together. This decision was in small part influenced by her desire to ensure that Hugh's way was clear to leave the country and study music at a proper academy.

It is during this time that she joined the National Council of African Women (NCAW), which was composed primarily of women like herself: professional, middle-class and church-going. She threw herself into the work of the NCAW and was away most weekends attending meetings all over the Reef and even beyond the Transvaal.

My father stopped sculpting altogether and went back to revisit his interest in penmanship, which he had learnt in teacher training at the Kilnerton Training Institution. But now he called it calligraphy. He began taking lessons from Mrs Mary Duxbury, who also taught at Polly Street Art Centre. He was reading Aldous Huxley and Lin Yutang and following the work of Frank Lloyd Wright, Picasso, Henry Moore and Alberto Giacometti. Ever enthused by design, he would take the time to explain the changes that were taking place in the arts, but at the centre of it all was his new interest in West African art, especially the masks. He was wistful, talking about the artists he knew personally who had left the country. Mancoba, Sekoto, he knew them well.

I never heard my father express a wish to go abroad. He loved being a South African, the one who remained at home. I wondered how he managed to keep himself in line and whether he did not wish that he too could get away. I wondered a great deal about my father and for a long time I was obsessed with incidents when he snapped into violence with Hugh and my mother, and once with me. I hated it when he wrote me a letter when I was in New York, apologising for slapping me when I was sixteen because I had slept at the house of close family friends, under supervision, after a wedding. I was embarrassed for him, wishing he had not brought it up after nearly three decades. It was so abject an apology, futile because it could never have undone that act of violence – and because it revealed to me that I had never been able to forgive the ones I loved the most and would suffer that assault afresh each time I was reminded about it by an apology.

Besides, I can always remember how he was the only one who taught me to observe. Searching became a way of life for me and I always found something new to entrance me. If we were travelling together in Johannesburg he would make a point of showing me something new. If we were driving together for whatever reason he would veer into Elm Street and take me to the hilltop of Munro Drive. I was always so frightened that the police would stop us but Papa, a very poor driver, would coax his old Wolseley to the peak of Munro Drive and park so that we could get out and view the scenery which, on a clear day, was a vast panorama of green with no Sandton skyscrapers, beyond which lay farmland, interspersed with koppies and bush and trees, giving way to a lush green, and far, far away on the horizon you could see the Magaliesberg under a blue sky daubed with cotton-wool clouds. On other occasions we would trudge our way through The Wilds, a magic garden with wondrous plants and trees, each with a name he lovingly enunciated as if he were a priest baptising a baby.

My father was mad for beauty and he stalked those who sought to express its secrets and messages. One of his favourite haunts was in Bramley, the studios of Edoardo Villa. He was occupied with calligraphy and creating citations, which he called Valedictory Addresses, from which he earned extra money. He would be commissioned to produce these formal addresses, written on special scrolls, in praise of departing public officials. He composed the tributes based on their CVs. They were couched in effusive terms of praise, honouring and acknowledging the officials' services. My mother did not succeed in persuading him to use simpler language, and one phrase that has stayed with me is 'the vicissitudes of life'. For all three of us it became a joke, at which my father laughed the loudest and which he would often use. But it was a very expensive business. The nibs, brushes and handmade paper were purchased in special art shops, and I still recall with great excitement the inks in all the colours of the rainbow and the metallic gold, silver and bronze.

For my father it was not enough to study European penman-ship – he had to explore Japanese, Chinese and Indian decorative writing as well. It did not matter that he could not read the languages; he was fascinated by the shapes of the scripts and the instruments that produced them. He was always at a distance from Western culture, but he delved more deeply into it as he retreated further into his own religious spirituality as a Lutheran layman.

I am hard put to describe my father's aesthetic, but whether it was a giraffe or a human he sculpted, he was always reaching out to something higher, something he would never find in the world in which he had chosen to live. As he grew older his figures lost their girth and grew more elongated as they lifted up to an unreachable height. So he continued to carve in wood, especially recycled wood, which forced its shape on him, dic-tating to him from its grain. He abandoned the stone of his first forays into art, leaving behind the nostalgia of the inimitable rocks of his Dikgale childhood – in the Great North, his name for what is now the Polokwane area – for the emaciated stick figures that grew ever thinner with the years.

When I considered the source of creativity I had to assert that there would always be a recurring possibility of two people, unknown to each other, living in different parts of the world, thinking of the same concept at the same time. One would receive accolades for it and get lucrative offers for it all over the world, while the other's renderings of a similar nature would be described as derivative. That is to say, my father read many books, knew many artists, and travelled in and out of varied aesthetic trends. He loved design from wherever it had come in the world. He loved the books of the world that showed gifted artists interpreting and revealing that world's beauty. He never had the luxury just to be single-mindedly creative. He was always distracted, mostly by the necessity of holding down jobs that did not leave enough time for his art.

Seeing examples of my father's art, I suspected that he could not squeeze his imagination into a single style because his mind roamed unrestricted and could not be contained in the township or in his rural past. He appropriated all design, whether it was about architecture, the landscape or the human body, and he was unapologetic about revelling in form. He was ravenous about design and all his books were covered with doodles, images straight from his imagination. I often wonder about his visits to the studio of Edoardo Villa and what he said to Lucas Legodi when he was there. My father was not a very formal man and would simply arrive unannounced at places, as if he had the right to be there. He did not carry the burden of Western protocol and as he grew older he became seized with seeing people from his past again, covering long distances in his bashed and battered car just to have a cup of tea and move on to his next host. It was a way of holding on to life for him.

He thought it a joke that the Dutch called his birthplace Zoekmekaar (look for one another), and because it made me laugh he never told me that in Setlokwa they called it Dikgale. I could never think about it, once he'd told me, without images of men, women and children on a perpetual search for one another. In a way my father was always searching, moving, changing, trying to find his metier in his artistic calling and in his personal life. So, from time to time, Linda Givon at the Goodman Gallery took his work to sell. Twenty-seven years later, when I had returned to South Africa and was always in a hurry and half-listening for the phone to ring, he told me that, in all the years for which I had been away, those sales were just enough for him to buy new materials to make more art.

No one kept a list of who had bought his art or where they had taken it. Elza Miles wrote about him in the 1993 FUBA Gallery Calendar and in her book *Land & Lives: A story of early black artists*, as did Steven Sack in *The Neglected Tradition: Towards a new history of South African art.* And when I met Dumile Feni in London for the first time, his eyes lit up as he stepped out of his studied posture, that of the angry artist, and told me, 'I know Uncle Tom. He is an inspiration. I know his work, which has inspired me.' I did not see his work at the Johannesburg Art Gallery — I believe it was stored in the basement — but when I met Mbulelo Mzamane for the first time in 1996, he told me, 'You must come and see your father's work at Fort Hare. It is in our collection.' I have not done so.

Yet I am angry and hurt that, like so many artists, he never fell into the limited quota of recognition lists. It is the norm to speculate what could have been, had the colour of his skin been different. But I prefer to wonder aloud what would have happened to his contemporaries, like Villa, Skotnes and Preller, had they been born African. My resentment lies there in my basket of recriminations, like his not having been able to leave me a building in downtown Johannesburg or a shop or a small plot near a river in the Magaliesberg. I wish he had been angrier about it when he was alive.

❖ ❖ ❖

THE BOLDNESS of the apartheid rulers was at all times acted out in the form of brazen mockery. They called our leaders 'agitators', as if their followers were an inert mass of inanimate ingredients floating in a pot, deaf and blind to their own lived experience of the fire burning beneath them. It was their speciality to call something one thing, when it was clearly another. They were like the puffed-up bully asking his puny victim, 'So, what are you going to do about it?' For instance, the Natives (Abolition of Passes and Co-ordination of Documents) Act of 1952 was in fact a more stringent application of the pass laws. There was no abolition, just an extension to women, for them to carry passes too!

Apartheid was on everybody's lips, although there was also talk about places like Ghana where Africans were about to rule themselves with the blessing of the British monarch. But it was the Mau Mau who captured the headlines. The British settlers were painted as innocent do-gooders at the mercy of blood-thirsty savages who had invented the latest form of atrocity. As the bloody independence unfolded in the Congo, we were gripped by newspaper accounts of what was characterised by the Western press as an inept melodrama among power-hungry protagonists motivated entirely by tribalism and self-interest. The articles dripped with the blood of innocent white martyrs slaughtered by wanton savages. Adoula, Kasavubu, Tshombe, all striving to ensure that Lumumba would not prevail. At the time, we did not know that this would become the motif of the unfolding decolonisation of Africa and beyond. Straw men, assassinations and the colonial retention of the economic high command.

My aunt had intervened decisively in the affair of my schooling. My mother had turned to her and together they cooked up the plan for me to attend the girls' seminary. I felt betrayed by my mother and resented Aunt Clara's agency in the whole matter. On the other hand, I realised that some sort of compromise had been reached, as my father had changed: he had become less autocratic. We even went together as a family to see Hugh perform in Trevor Huddleston's Huddleston Jazz Band at the Wits University Great Hall. Hugh was yet a fledgling in the music world, but his membership of the band was earning frequent mentions in the newspapers, and Papa graciously stepped into the role of proud father.

My mother's repulsion for Bantu education never wavered and later, in 1960, as I was about to leave Inanda, I was able to stand up to my father and refuse to go to Turfloop University in the Great North. It was the same year in which Hugh left South Africa to study music in London. Two years before, as I had approached my Junior Certificate examinations, I had failed to convince my father to let me transfer from Inanda so that I could do matric at Kilnerton Training Institution in Pretoria, nearer home. By then I was seeing my parents in a decidedly less romantic light. We were all just here in South Africa trying to make our way in a difficult time for all black people and I had begun to realise that I was on my own.

I was drunk with rejection and feelings of abandonment when I went to Inanda. I could not understand why, after only four years, they could so fickly send me away, so far away again. My father had rejected all other alternatives of day schools near-by, especially Madibane High School in Newclare, which had the best results in the country. My cousin Pothinius Mokgokong had a reputation as a brilliant English teacher, and he taught there, which made no difference to my father. Others, children of my father's friends like Jiyane Mbere and Roseinnes Phahle, had gone there and excelled, but my father would not budge.

I noticed that Mama had become bolder in challenging my father's view in matters regarding our upbringing, and that the move to Alexandra had made her more outspoken and unafraid to stand up to him. Her anger about the fiasco of her participation in the Defiance Campaign in 1952 had never burnt out. It lay smouldering and fuelled by the frequent newspaper reports of women's growing militancy all over the country. The names of women like Dora Tamana, Josie Palmer, Annie Silinga and Lillian Ngoyi were prominent in accounts of the defiance against the pass laws, and at the Entokozweni Family Centre my mother's director Helen Navid drew many of her comrades into support work for the centre. It was here that she met Monty and Myrtle Berman, who were to become foster parents to Hugh during the rehearsals for *King Kong*: he could not come home after rehearsals for fear of arrest under the pass laws, which included a strict curfew.

A staunch admirer of Josie Palmer, my mother, thwarted in her zeal to be a part of the overtly political struggle, joined the NCAW, the organisation for enlightened mothers that abjured overt political activism in favour of social upliftment. But it was the discovery of the sale of the Lady Selborne property that stoked her fury. My parents had purchased the stand when they had first moved to Alexandra, when they still had a joint bank account. It was their dream to build a house there and own something for the future. Now it was all gone without an acknowledgement of her part-ownership because, like all black females, she had no rights to property. She was a minor in law; her husband had the authority to dispose of what they owned jointly and she was without recourse. It did not matter that she was a qualified professional with a responsible job. She was now just as powerless as her social work 'cases'.

Amidst all the national and personal drama, my sister Sybil was born on 29 July 1954. Like all older female children in African families, I now had the responsibility of assisting my mother to look after her, which I did grudgingly. At this point my grand-mother was still living with us, but already making arrangements to move to her new house. My mother took maternity leave but was keen to get back to work after three months. She would only be able to take Sybil to work when Sybil was old enough to enter the nursery school. So Auntie Tinnie came to live with us in Alexandra and to help my mother, again.

✧ ✧ ✧

THE 1954 Annual Report of Entokozweni Family Centre, un-der the directorship of Helen Navid, is an example of a radical approach to social work that has yet to be matched in present-day South Africa. Interestingly, the majority of the staff were women. The programmes of the centre had an integrated approach that spanned the disciplines of medicine, education, labour, family economics and sport. At first, they targeted small family groups in the vicinity of the centre, but as their effectiveness grew, they had to be extended to the community as a whole. Alexandra was an important site of the political struggle and the ANC was well entrenched there. Leaders like Sisulu and Mandela, and Father Trevor Huddleston, were frequent visitors at Entokozweni. The Social Medicine project was led by two medical couples who were admirers of the Sidney Kark Pholela project in Natal. They were strong allies of Helen Navid, and when she was banned they refused to take a low profile, in defence of the political activities she had espoused. All were openly associated with the Congress of Democrats, a radical white anti-apartheid group that was part of the Congress Alliance, and worked hand in hand with Helen Navid. At the time, Huddleston was also spearheading the resistance to the removal of Sophiatown and the closure of St Peter's Secondary School.

A significant portion of the funding for the centre was raised by Wits University students in the annual university rag. On that first Saturday in spring, Wits students took over the city routes leading to and from Alexandra. Dressed in attention-seeking costumes and bizarre clown make-up, they took over Johannesburg, collecting money for Entokozweni Family Centre. The close network of cooperation, which included the Alexandra Health Committee, Wits Medical School, Alexandra Clinic, the Jan H Hofmeyr School of Social Work and the African National Congress, inevitably led to a direct clash with the apartheid authorities, who first named, then banned, Helen Navid in 1955. Among the leading actors in the centre's Social Medicine project were Mervyn Susser, Zena Stein, Michael Hathorn and Margaret Cormack, all political activists and leading medical scientists who subsequently had to leave South Africa under threat of political persecution. The surveys, research and immunisation projects in cancer, typhoid fever, diphtheria and tuberculosis were organised in concert with Dr AB Xuma, the Medical Officer of Health at the Alexandra Health Committee, where my father worked as the part of the health inspectorate. The inspectorate included Alfred Nzo, who was to become the longest-serving secretary general of the ANC in exile and first foreign minister in the new democratic government of 1994.

One cannot but imagine what could have happened had this integrated experiment in social medicine been sustained, or had it been tried in the new South Africa. The centre had a nutrition clinic, vegetable club, primary school (that had its classes, at first, in the open air), boys' club, girls' club, and sewing and cookery classes, as well as a recreational programme, which showed films on a regular basis. Entokozweni had a black staff of over thirty, including six social workers, nursing sisters, nursery school teachers, a domestic science teacher, a sports master and four primary school teachers, complemented by a boxing instructor.

This was the milieu of my parents' professional life. They learnt and shared the same values in community service, and they were exposed to the leading practitioners and the most radical medical and social intellectuals and activists of the era. For Mama, raised in KwaGuqa in a tavern, this exposure translated into a political activism that would be thwarted by custom, tradition and fear, and for my father, the son of a Lutheran evangelist, it led to a deeper commitment to his calling as a sculptor in a world where Africans could never attain recognition beyond servitude.

❖ ❖ ❖

THE SINGLE durable memory of my year at the City and Suburban Coloured School is of my English teacher, a Mr John Braam. He was a university graduate and definitely did not come from Newclare or Doornfontein. His navy-blue blazer, pressed grey flannel pants and white shirt spoke of elite Coronationville or some other such coloured enclave, where men did not work in the factory or do any manual work except gardening and maybe carpentry as a hobby. He was different from my rough-and-ready uncles who still lived in Doornfontein, on Sivewright Avenue.

I was the only child from Alexandra at the school and Mr Braam would make sure I left school in time to catch my bus before the rush hour. He had noticed me from my good grades in English and arithmetic. A sober man with a side parting in his hair and highly polished brown leather shoes, he came to my rescue when the authorities in Pretoria demanded birth certificates from all the registered pupils. We were about to write the half-year examinations when Pretoria pounced, demanding that pupils submit birth certificates to prove that we were coloured, neither native nor white.

I remember going to Braam's office after weeks of evasion. I walked in and blurted out everything. My father is African. His name is Masekela. I have no coloured birth certificate. I did not even realise I was crying as he proffered a white handkerchief from his jacket pocket. He patted me on the shoulder and told me not to worry. 'You will be able to write your examinations and no one is going to stop you.' Everything else about that year is a blur – the buildings, the teachers and pupils, all interred in a deep hole, sealed and obliterated by the landmark political events that took me there and brought me back to where I would discard the surname Maskell to become, once more, a Masekela.

In a haunting sense, 1955 was a year I erased from reference. Unlike the unprecedented political events of that decade, the coloured school is a faded splotch, an ink stain on a much-laundered white shirt, which only the launderer and the owner can see when they choose to find it. I regard the events of that year as a kind of temporary sleepwalking. I was like a somnolent stroller, aware of all the obstacles in my path yet able to return safely to the comfort of my bed, in the morning denying with vigour that I had ever wandered off in my sleep.

But what happened to me that year does not matter in the greater scheme of the unprecedented events of that decade. My experience was merely a petty episode at a time when our erstwhile rulers were setting in place a plan for a permanent solution to shut down all opposition to white domination. Already an avid reader, I had read about the Nazi era in the popular *Reader's Digest* that my father purchased regularly. But it was the serialised *The Diary of Anne Frank* that both chilled and riveted me. Her capture by the Nazis after months of hiding in an empty house fixed in me a dread of leather boots and military uniforms. In our home there many books and magazines and I for one had followed the adventures of Mr Drum, Henry Nxumalo, the great investigative journalist, exposing the slave conditions on a Bethal potato farm and the living conditions of African prisoners.

I was disturbed by the description of native reserves and the frequent reference to their similarities to concentration camps. The frequent executions, especially at Pretoria Central Prison, were often splashed on the front pages of the Sunday papers, and I could not forget Uncle Bower's brutal death in Brakpan. A seed of fear had been planted in my head when my uncle had been beaten to death by those three white racist youths. But now I was living in one of the most dangerous townships in the country, with a true and tested polity that had successfully sustained two historically unprecedented bus boycotts. The No. 2 Square near the PUTCO bus terminus was the venue for many public meetings of the ANC. Whenever I could get away on Sunday mornings, like other youth, I would hang around the edges of political gatherings, and even the crackling loudspeakers set up near the podium could not swallow up our roaring *iAfrika!* in response to the raised fist and the call *Mayibuye!* The voice from the podium could very well be Sisulu's, Mandela's, or our local firebrand Sidzumo's. The political organisations were still legal, and operated in the open − as did the Special Branch of the police, who were always taking notes and photographs at the meetings.

It was then that I was told for the first time that I would be sent away to Inanda. I had no idea that for the next five years the only privacy I would get there would be when I was reading a book in the library.

Auntie Clara, a nursing sister at McCord Zulu Hospital, had instigated this move. In my uncle's words, she and my father had 'plotted and schemed' to outmanoeuvre Mama's carefully laid plans for me to escape Bantu Education. They had conspired and engineered the whole Inanda project right under my mother's nose, he insisted. In fact, it was Mama who had turned to Auntie Clara for help. The Coloured School plans had gone awry. The apartheid authorities were a step ahead, as had been shown by the demand for birth certificates, and some of the school authorities were only too eager to comply with Pretoria.

Mr John Braam was not. Failure to produce one would have meant that I could not write the Standard Six examinations and proceed to high school. The government was intent on closing all the loopholes for migration from one racial category to another. Gazetted law stated that a coloured person had to prove that they were not white or native. Obviously, I would never succeed in getting into a coloured high school now, so my entire educational future was in jeopardy.

My father distanced himself from the whole 'catastrophe', pleading that he had agreed to the plan for the sake of domestic peace. This was not surprising: many of my paternal relatives had expressed their disquiet about his allowing what they considered a travesty, a denial of his traditional position as head of his family. Obviously, her mixed-raced background placed Mama on the back foot. Despite all evidence to the contrary, she was now suspected of harbouring racial motives. Yet the whole issue had never been a secret. She had made a rational decision that would not only have me avoid an extra year in school, but also enable me to enter an open university before the so-called Extension of University Education Act became law.

No one could counter her argument that Bantu Education was inferior. All over the country teachers were condemning it, and even losing their jobs by publicly demonstrating their hatred of the scheme. Even some of our family friends and relatives who were now sub-inspectors in the system abhorred it, but as has been the case with the majority of those deemed 'successful' throughout history, they chose stability over risk-ing the meagre rewards of middle-class life. Unlike Ezekiel Mphahlele, Livingstone Mqotsi and many others all over the country who made their opposition public and lost their jobs, they remained within the system and played a continuing role in the education of the young.

Inanda Seminary School and McCord Zulu Hospital had both been run by the American Board of Missions since the abolition of slavery in the nineteenth century. Daniel and Lucy Lindley arrived in South Africa in 1834 and founded Inanda Seminary in 1869 to provide appropriate helpmeets who would comple-ment the evangelistic work carried out by the growing number of young African male missionaries trained at Adams College. The emphasis of the school's training was on religious studies and domestic skills. It became well known for its high academic standards and rigorous moral training, and was recognised in particular as an institution for the training of young African women by women missionaries.

When the Bantu Education Act of 1953 aimed to entrench complete control of all aspects of African education, in particular the content of the curriculum, Africans had to sit for their own examinations based on a separate curriculum and different cri-teria. Dr Lavinia Scott, Inanda's principal, fought a meritorious battle to retain the excellent standards of the school while reject-ing Bantu Education for as long as it was feasible to do so. As it was, my class of 1960 was the last group to sit for the common Joint Matriculation Board examination.

Auntie Clara had enjoyed a fulfilling professional experience working with the missionary Dr Alan Taylor, who was head of the hospital. She may have entertained some hopes that I would also enter the nursing profession, but mainly she was keen to have me under the tutelage of the Americans, whose approach contrasted markedly with her Lutheran background, as well as with the Church of Scotland Mission training she had received at Lovedale. It now makes sense that she chose Inanda for me. She wanted to expose me to a wider world in the same way that she had dared to study in faraway Alice in the Eastern Cape rather than stay cooped up in the narrow confines of her family. She wanted me to spread my wings and be opened up to a different experience. For most elders during that period, when we did not even utter words like 'vagina', 'penis', 'sex', or 'orgasm', the overriding reason for boarding school was to protect young women from pregnancy and the other destructive social dangers looming in the townships. By all accounts my aunt had succeeded brilliantly in her career, even gaining promotion to the position of senior nursing sister at McCord Hospital. I remember her coming to KwaGuqa to play competitive tennis in a tournament once. For that weekend she was our guest, sleeping in the front room that was reserved for visitors.

To this day I am filled with awe by the story of how she made a bonfire of my grandfather's old working clothes. On vacation in Walmansthal once, she was dismayed to see the ragged condition of his work clothes. Since all her siblings were employed and all sent a monthly contribution for their parents' upkeep, she tackled him about his tattered look, to no avail. With the help of my grandmother she collected all his old clothes, pretending she was going to patch them up. She waited until he was bathing so that she could add what he had taken off to the bundle. He shuffled to his bedroom in his dressing gown to find new clothes laid out on the bed for him. Surprised and angered by this unexpected turn in the order of his life, he rushed out of his bedroom, calling to his wife.

Instead, it was Clara who responded, 'I am the one who took your clothes and I am burning them. You are a disgrace, going around in rags as though we don't support you.'

My grandmother, her lips pursed tight, stood at the door motionless, watching my aunt holding a long stick to the fire under the moonlit sky. One by one, she threw his tattered clothes into the blaze.

Calmly, she turned the flaming rags on the bonfire: 'Yes, I am burning these rags. From tomorrow onwards, you will no longer parade around, shaming us, as a ragged beggar!'

All my grandfather could do was repeat, 'Clara! Clara!' as he shuffled back to his bedroom. In that audacious act of brazen arson, his daughter had chipped away more of his unquestioned authority over the family.

My aunt had a way of implementing her thoughts before they could be questioned. It was not unusual for her to force stuck windows open to let fresh air in for a newborn baby (a no-no in African circles, where a baby could be swaddled in blankets even when it was torrid outside and only exposed to the outside environment at three months old), or to change the position of the furniture in our house while my mother was at work. The changes she made tended to be improvements. My mother admired her and loved her because she was 'progressive', and she never argued with Clara. She would just wait until Clara had returned to Natal, then change everything back to where it had been. But when Clara came for another visit, her changes would be reinstated before she arrived.

I guess it was the same with my landing up at Inanda: my mother embraced it because she realised how much the year at the Coloured School had changed me. I had carried the aloofness of the school day over to the evenings at home as I secretly battled with the personal humiliation and shame. I could not speak out to either of my parents. I had to put up a front to keep clear of the marital push and pull at home. I could not find the words to convey the subtleties of the slights and rebuffs.

I was also growing older, and it irked me when remarks were made about my body. Some people even went as far as saying that I was growing into a beauty just like my mother. It was a lie, as she was without physical blemish in every way. I already understood that I wanted a different life from hers and that, whether I desired it or not, Inanda Seminary was the place that had been chosen for the next five years of my life. At the Coloured School I was nothing because of my kinky hair. Alone at home I stared at myself in the mirror, brooding over my moon face and sharply pointed chin that seemed to invite touching.

Papa asked, 'Why is she so sour?'

Mama replied, 'It is growing pains. At boarding school she will adjust in the company of her peers.'

My parents spoke like that more and more often, in the textbook language of their professional work. Their view of the world was influenced by more than their immediate whereabouts. They strained to reach out to the possibilities beyond the many boundaries that apartheid was constructing everywhere, among race groups, in the cities, the towns and the rural areas. In retrospect, I have never ceased to appreciate Auntie Clara's forwardness and decisiveness in thrusting me into an environment whose sameness provided the foil for a clearer and a broader picture beyond my immediate family – and far enough away from the patriarchal spirit that ruled, then, and still rules, now, every nook and cranny of South African life, irrespective of race, creed or colour.

Also in retrospect – now, in my eighth decade – I remember that as a child in KwaGuqa even parts of my body were remarked on as belonging to different members of my family, some of whom I had never even met. It gave me a sense of belonging that I held the power to evoke the presence of beloved others whom I would never know. At the same time, it detracted from my own sense of ownership of my self. The authority of the self-appointed observers was intrusive, especially when they went on to argue among themselves, fixing me in the lens of their own visions. It dismembered me. To this day, I am Jwana as I am Kenneth as I am Rakgadi Mokonye, whom we called the Sphinx. However, with the help of experience and unplanned encounters, I am also the girl from Haiti with the green eyes and the blonde, kinky hair who was mother to my son, Mabusha, in LA. I am Krotoa and Mmanthatisi and Delilah and Auntie Pixie.

My orphan Auntie Pixie, who could not read, who could not write, who knew not mother or father, whose sister was named Trixie to rhyme with Pixie, whose squinch eyes were ever-moving, always wary. Auntie Pixie was our adopted aunt, brought to us by Uncle Bigvai, who found her in Modderfontein where he was a mine clerk. Mr Malan, my uncle's supervisor, had inherited Auntie Pixie from his father. His father had brought her back from South West Africa as part of the World War I booty in 1915, when the German colony had been conquered by South African troops.

By the time I went to Inanda, Auntie Pixie was in the employ of the Cooper family in Dunkeld. Mrs Cooper had taught her haute cuisine and patisserie. She knew how to darn socks and the correct temperatures at which to launder all the varieties of textiles, which ones to starch and what others to dry flat on the ground. Her employers took her with them to England and to France when they went on vacation so she could look after their babies when they went out to restaurants and theatres, or if they opted to treat the children to fresh air in the children's playground in the park.

She was an expert at making sandwiches and knew how to pack them in the cane basket and knew all about flasks for hot and cold drinks. At the beach she ensured that she handed out the correct towel or serviette to members of the family, anticipating their every need without intruding on their privacy. Trixie died at ten years old, and from then on Auntie Pixie was always alone with the Malans, then with the Coopers. She could speak only Afrikaans and broken English. At least they had taught her to sign her name on her passport. She supervised the work of the 'garden boy' and fed him leftovers as instructed, and once or twice a week he came into the house to wash the windows, to scrub and polish the floors, to empty the ashes from the fireplace. She had no isiZulu, Sesotho or siSwati and her communication was limited to matters pertaining to the feeding, the dressing and everything connected to the convenience of the Malans and Coopers until she was in her early forties. She was still a virgin.

I was about eleven when I first met her. By then she had been fully adopted by the greater Masekela family. In particular, the social worker in my mother embraced Auntie Pixie, and it was not long before Mama had insinuated herself into Mrs Cooper's business, convincing her that Auntie Pixie needed some days off every month to spend the weekend with us. By the time I went off to Inanda, Auntie Pixie would spend at least one night per month at our house in Alex.

When I returned for the July holidays she had been 'scarce' and had brought a gentleman friend with her on her last day visit. Mrs Cooper was full of complaints about the hours she kept and how she was now answering back. In my second year at Inanda, the Coopers fired Auntie Pixie because she was found to be pregnant. She went to live with Ouma in Grasmere until the house she was building for herself there was completed. At about forty-five she gave birth to her only child and raised him in Grasmere. She never went back to work as she had saved enough money to take care of herself.

The enormity of Auntie Pixie's life in my view is beyond

analysis. She always carried with her that child in the cave, hiding with her sister from the loud noises of the guns of war. They were just a screaming mess of a bundle when they were found in that cave. She only knew the place was called Damaraland, but she spoke no Damara. Caribib, she called herself. Pixie Caribib. She was my aunt.

There are more in the constellation of humanity that has brought me here and each one of them is a link in the chain that binds me together.

I HAD never heard any of my father's family speak ill of Ouma, but I know that, since I had been raised in a shebeen, with an interval in a crime-ridden township followed by a year as a coloured, it was now time for me to be placed in a more elevating environment where I could be exposed to a higher purpose in life. Nothing could erase Ouma's reputation as an independent home brewer who had built her house and educated her daughter from the proceeds of alcoholic beer she sold to mine workers. Worse still, she had travelled widely and knew dangerous places like Kimberley and Lydenburg and she had the physical strength to defend herself in a fight with any man who dared to challenge her on her premises.

The glaring gap in her life would always be Walter Bower. In a divided society dominated by men, this being a woman alone, this surviving and raising your children single-handedly, this shoving misbehaving drinkers out of your house and through the gate, this holding your own keys, was why, in the reports from commissions about the native problem, women of her ilk were labelled as 'carriers of disease', 'loose women', and so on. The plan had always been to capture African male labour. Under the circumstances, the presence of black women was an unintended consequence and a nuisance.

Later on, with growing industrialisation, it was the white women, the rural poor, who would dominate the workplace because they could be paid less than the white men. Black women were still the lowest on the totem pole of workers, eking out a living as domestic workers for the growing new white working classes in the cities and towns. They fought poverty and ensured the education of their children by doing washing, nannying, cleaning and cooking. But the reputation of 'looseness' clung to them and by the 1950s, under apartheid, they were considered 'superfluous appendages'. Others, like Ouma, preferred to be self-employed, brewing and selling alcohol. Popular culture would have us believe in the hardened stereotype of what became known as the shebeen queen. In fact, alcohol and its manufacture has historically been a factor in South African life and the management of black labour.

IN THE widening political repression unfolding in the country, it was not possible to imagine that things could get worse. The imperative, then, was not the building of monuments to suffering; increasingly, all that was available was the means to maintain the stability of home. It was not a time to weigh and measure who suffered more than whom and who deserved which prizes and rewards and how many perks. Retail therapy was not even a notion. Our celebrities were local, like the nurses in their bright, white, starched uniforms with maroon epaulettes. Celebrity was not a commodity that you could buy or sell, and when a man was executed in Pretoria we were reminded solemnly that he was the child of a woman somewhere. Nostalgia was selective, and everybody was an uncongratulated hero in their own sphere for being witty, for singing at church, for being able to find the BBC or the Lourenço Marques station on the crackling radio.

In KwaGuqa, in Mamelodi, in the tattered squatting communities of every town, it was the spirit of survival that mattered. Johanna and her peers, all of whom had seen the unspeakable, actively exorcised the past by fashioning a present for us. Every day they allowed themselves to wonder at the risen sun beaming from the same blue heavens as yesterday. It was the stuff of plain human endurance. In this there was a merciful inclination towards wresting laughter from the most humiliating circumstances. There were jokes galore about lying and grovelling to white policemen on patrol to arrest black men under the pass laws. The first word out of the mouth of the policeman was always 'kaffir' and the practised response of his prey was an automatic '*my baas*' (my boss). It helped to get you where you were heading.

No black preacher, no teacher, no ordinary working man was spared from explaining why and how he had come to be where he was, in the white man's town. Reaching for the page of the passbook that held the monthly signature of your employer was a reflex action when you saw a policeman. And God help you if you were driving a car loaded with your wife and children on a deserted road after sunset. Then you might still have to explain why you were so slow in getting out of the car, why your hat was still on your head and your eyes not on your feet. If you averted your eyes it irritated them and when you looked them in the eye it filled them with fury. If they let you go you collected yourself and deposited yourself on the driver's seat hoping they would not suddenly remember something else they had forgotten to ask you about. There was no guarantee that you would not be stopped again after a few miles.

Mercifully, the age of police radios had not yet arrived.

At times, even when you were dismissed to hurry to where you were heading, the police car would tail you for some miles then abruptly make a U-turn and drive away in a cloud of dust. In your car, driving on again, there would be a fleeting silence – an angel passing, as we used to say – until someone made a joke of it and you all laughed, eager to erase the image of this man in the car with you, your father, your husband, your brother or your son who had just been reduced to a kaffir and a boy.

I grew up long before this age of outing. Talk was not glib, nor expressions tailored to select words concealing actuality. The straitjacket of political correctness had not yet been designed. In the circumstances of daily public humiliation, of indignity and brute force piled on the black population, there emerged wit, humour and plain human forbearance. Unlike what had happened to Ouma and Ouma Sussie and all those others born in earlier bondage, there were more voices every day, not only of our own kith and kin, who were declaring, in their own tongue, a version of 'Come back, Africa'. We learnt that our Sisulus, Mandelas, Dadoos were not servile agitators merely stoking terrorist fires at the behest of Iron Curtain puppeteers, but that they had like-minded peers with exotic names like Kwame Nkrumah, Jomo Kenyatta, Julius Nyerere and Patrice Lumumba. Yet unschooled in the subtleties of metaphoric expression, my young mind was stretched by the meaning of phrases like 'Cold War'. It was just as confounding as my attempts to imagine the enormity of a vast 'Iron Curtain' barring people from one another, yet I lived in a place whose minority white rulers sought in every way possible to screen themselves off from the reality of a majority that would always prevail unless it was destroyed.

Stripped, deprived, detained in solitary confinement, tortured, banished, exiled, shot and killed, tried for treason, forcibly removed, jailed, executed, silenced, eliminated, named, confined –

these became the everyday words on the lips of the country, said in factories, on the mines, in courts, in schools, in churches, in buses and trains and over the fence. This was not an attempt to destroy the social fabric of African life, it was a full-fledged project intended to entrench permanent *baasskap*. It would, in fact, result in the dismembering of our society in physical terms, in transplanting large groups of people into unproductive geographical areas devoid of the most basic conveniences they had seen in the cities from which they had been expelled.

What was even more rankling is that, from the times of their first encounters with Europeans, blacks had been compelled by material conditions to view themselves in relation to what they had helped to create with their labour but which they would never own. So, when we said as children to each other in anger, '*Uzenz'umlungu*' (You're acting like a white person), it was the most cutting of insults – even though we did not fully comprehend the ramifications of the insult.

JUST AFTER Ouma and I had moved to Alexandra and Hugh had gone to St Peter's as a boarder, a boy older than him was brought home by my father. It was soon after my grandfather's death and Mamoshaba, my grandmother, was now living in Springs at my uncle's house. His name was Duggie and unlike all the children who had been my mother's 'cases' he was there to stay. He took my place on the studio couch, my bed, and I was now to share a bedroom with Ouma and Elaine.

Accustomed as I was to having displaced children living temporarily with us, and already preoccupied with my new school in town, I paid scant attention to his presence. I soon gathered that he was the cause for the loud quarrels between my parents. Long after the candles had been blown out, when the night-soil men had come and gone, I heard my mother say, 'He must go back to where he came from.' My mother greeted him politely, he was fed and clothed, but he was set apart from us by not being given house tasks. He just sat there, occasionally going to the front gate, staring up and down the street.

With my grandfather deceased and my paternal grandmother Mamoshaba gone to live at Uncle Kenneth's, Ouma took the sudden arrival of Duggie as a personal slight. She concluded that my father was really disrespecting her and daring her to leave his house. As usual, I sympathised with everyone's point of view, but in particular my heart went out to Duggie. I envied Hugh and now also wished that I could go away. Undoubtedly, it set Ouma on her long-threatened way out, to live on her own.

My mother wondered aloud why my father was always out late and not spending time with Duggie. It called for a family indaba. This time, it was all my father's siblings who came to lay down the law. They all came, except Rakgadi Mokonye. Kenneth concluded that she had a hand in the Duggie matter, hence her absence. The big family discussion was presided over by my Aunt Johanna Lekgetha. Unlike the discussion about her participation in the Defiance Campaign, this time my mother won and Duggie left.

I was to meet him again when I returned home from exile in 1990. My sisters and I went to a lunch he had organised to welcome me at his home in Mamelodi. We never referred to his short stint in our Alexandra home, but now, almost fifty and still by myself and a single mother of two sons, I secretly brooded over that sad, unwanted boy I had met nearly forty years ago in Alexandra. He, like millions of young men, had been raised by a single mother who instilled in him the love of all family as legitimate. Central to everything was recognition by your father and his family.

It was a crowded time, just before I went to Inanda. Four

years had passed since I had come to live in Alexandra. Hugh was still the centre of attraction, but more so now for having gone astray. He had flouted my father's wishes. His choice to become a musician had dented Papa's expectations that his firstborn son would become the first medical doctor in the Masekela family. His academic performance at St Peter's had been dismal, resulting in failure in his second year. It strained the fragile peace that had come with Sybil's birth. I had now been turned into Papa's great hope and all his attention was fixed on me. I became the bridge that connected my parents, crossing the lines to bear good news in both directions, learning to be the diplomat, seeing both sides of the story, as well as my own.

Five years was how long I was to spend at Inanda, a whole year longer than the time I had spent living with both of my parents for the first time. All of us, old and new girls, started counting the days until the winter holidays in June from the day of our arrival in January. After everything I had been through with Ouma in KwaGuqa, in Alexandra under my father's roof and for the whole year at the Coloured School, Inanda was at first merely just a new home whose formalities I would get to know in time. But that first morning at the communal bathroom rocked all my foundations about modesty and privacy.

Each of us carried a cleaned chamber pot with cold water and placed it on a long rack from one end of the room to the other. The room was filled with girls from about thirteen to nineteen years old, all in some form of undress. Some were leaving the room almost dressed, others were just entering, some with a towel on the shoulder or around the waist, and the rest were hurriedly washing their naked bodies with the water in their chamber pots. There was a murmur of easy conversation among the older girls and it was all I could do not to gape at this mass exhibition of live, naked shapes, all at different stages of their ablution and racing to get out of that draughty, ill-lit room.

I was ill at ease, unaccustomed to revealing my body freely. It was not done where I came from – where you had to sit with your legs together and the parting of legs in any posture was for men only. I was raised to ensure that my private parts were covered, that girls did not part their legs in sitting on the ground or on a chair, that they did not lie on their backs warming in the sun. This mass abandon of breasts and pubic hair, spare and abundant, all on display, was staggering. Since everybody else seemed to take it in their stride, I moved along with the rest, pretending that I was at ease. I do not recall ever discussing it at home or with any of the other new girls. But it was an assault on my senses, a psychic ambush I was too young to understand.

I thought about it when Ouma was gravely ill. It was almost three years after my return from twenty-seven years of exile. Ouma was dying but she struggled with all her waning might to keep me from washing her between her legs. With my sister's help, we held her down and I reached in there with a wet soapy cloth, then rinsed her with warm, clean water. Tears of impotence raced down her face as I patted her dry with a clean towel. It was just before she was admitted to hospital for the first and only time at a hundred and four years old, with a gangrenous toe. I was both sad and angry with her as she sputtered, 'Disrespectful! It is not done. My nakedness is not a child's plaything!'

In all those years for which we had shared a bedroom, I had never seen Ouma's naked body. Now at Inanda I was assailed by mass nudity, lines of girls splashing water on their nakedness, indifferent to my prying eyes. At home, undressing required the practised agility of an athlete. Somehow it was not considered so bad if your naked back was seen. I guess it is because male and female are similar from the back. So, the first rule was to turn your back to whoever was in the room.

In between the casual conversation the girls washed between their legs, some drying the skin under their pendulous breasts, yet others patting dry between their buttocks. But it was the skin on their faces that took up scrutiny in the tiny mirrors we had all brought with us from home.

'Wash behind your ears! Put that soapy rag between your legs!' These orders were barked out randomly to the freshers from some of the older girls, a few bullies who longed for the extreme hazing ways that were not allowed at Inanda. My eyes wandered down the long row of chamber pots and the line of young women totally engaged in finishing their wash in time for breakfast and totally disinterested in the nudity that had me mesmerised. The only nakedness I knew was of babies and the undressedness of sexual intercourse I had read about from the book in my mother's bedside table drawer. In the crowded living conditions of African family life in the locations, my family had a strict protocol about covering the body, and children were not supposed to see the naked bodies of adults. It was January, and summer, and I could not imagine how I would hold up washing from a chamber pot of colder water in winter in June. I envied the girls from Durban and the surrounding areas. They had regular visitors who brought them food and fruit, while those of us from the other provinces depended on our tinned goods that got depleted long before the middle of the term. I wondered whether the teachers knew the conditions of our bathrooms and the food we ate. I wrote formal letters to my parents, stripped of all emotion and giving a summary of my school activities.

❖ ❖ ❖

BY THE time I left for Inanda in 1956, my father's application to the Natalspruit Municipality had been successful and

Mama's application for a position as a social worker was under consideration. Her first prize would have been to work for the Johannesburg Social Welfare Department but her matrimonial responsibility was to follow her husband. Ouma's house in Grasmere was ready and Sybil and Elaine would be moving there with her until my parents settled down in Natalspruit. This year would be a major transition for everyone in my troubled family.

I would never forgive my parents for sending me to boarding school. For my first holidays home that winter I went to 1419 Nhlapo Section in Natalspruit, our new home. The house, which looked exactly like every other four-roomed house on the street, was much smaller than the one in 12th Avenue in Alexandra had been. Hovering over the house was a model of an eight-legged insect-like creature wrought with thick wire, resting on a bed of dark, smooth pebbles. My father, a tall, hefty man, could not enter the front door without stooping.

My mother had not warned me about any of these changes and watched my reaction with amusement as we entered the house. It was like a doll's house, all done up with low furniture in what my father explained was Japanese style designed for small spaces. Hugh was away, on the road; Ouma was in Grasmere with my two sisters. It was just me and my parents, and it felt awfully close.

Nothing stays neatly ordered. I would change, as would my parents and all the places and people I had known, my brother would leave and go far away, abroad where I could not see him, but Inanda would remain the same. It would always be the pottery wheel out of whose revolution would emerge newly formed vessels, each one of the same clay, fired in the same kiln to emerge with the unique signature of the maker.

It was heart-wrenching to part with my parents again.

'Your father thinks it best for you,' Mama said as I sat between her knees, my legs outstretched on the kitchen floor. The pots were cooking. She sat on the round wooden footstool my father had carved for her, dressing my hair, parting it in the middle and pulling the comb through it. Unlike hers, my hair shrank like wool when it had been washed and it had to be coaxed with a pomade to separate the kinks. It was an ordeal to put the comb through it and it had to be braided while it was still damp. At times the braids were so tight that even smiling was difficult for a few days afterwards and the skin at the roots around the partings got inflamed.

Still, it was a special ritual, this unravelling, this painful rite to smooth out what was rough, to flatten what was uneven. We were facing the same way and she had to bow her head a bit and hold my head still between her legs to stop me from wriggling. I could not see her face but I knew it by heart and it was drawn there in fervent shades of a felt devotion. Those lines around her worried brow, the measured impatience from broken promises and the sheer weight of not being able to shape the path ahead were all in my mind-portrait of my mother. That is what I took with me to Inanda. Sometimes in the many years of exile in Ghana, in Zambia, in London and in the US, I would laugh out loud and hear the tinkle of the notes of my mother's mirth in my own.

The tones of her unspoken feelings still pour out inside me and my eyes smart. I tilt my head back as if balancing a ball on the rounded tip of my nose, just like she used to do to show strength, and like her I swallow my tears.

✦✦✦

I WAS morose and sulky for weeks as my departure to boarding school was discussed. In typical fashion in our extended family, it seemed like every one of them had their own view about my future, each one different from mine. Only Uncle Kenny, my father's youngest brother, sympathised with me. He also reasoned with me, saying that after five years at Inanda no one would ever have the nerve to order me to do anything I did not want to do.

I would be my own woman.

Uncle Kenny was the black sheep of the Masekela family, having been expelled from the Kilnerton Training Institution for denying the existence of the Christian God. The philosophical debate in the lecture room morphed into an altercation with the lecturer. He carried his expulsion like a badge of honour for the rest of his life. The last-born in his family, he had been coddled by his three sisters and two brothers, especially his sister and best friend, Clara. She had fled the family coop to study nursing in Alice, near Fort Hare, rejecting the option of studying nearer home.

Clara had scrimped and saved, and she had finally managed to pay for his enrolment at Kilnerton.

On leaving Kilnerton, Uncle Kenny had refused to return to Walmansthal, where my grandfather was now retired and still living on the farm where he had been a teacher and an evangelist. Uncle Kenny opted to live with the newly married couple, my mother and father, who had just welcomed Hugh, their first baby. Uncle Kenneth always got his way. Five years younger than my mother, he helped her navigate her way into the affections of her new family because he knew them best and did not fear any of them. His irreverence was matched only by his ability to reduce all of them to tears of laughter.

Even my aunt Rakgadi Mokonye, the Sphinx, would momentarily spread her lips into a reluctant smile of disapproval when he recalled their past on the three different mission stations, where growing up was a mere incident on the path of service to others. As much as her siblings threw themselves carelessly into nostalgia, she buried herself in her knitting and crocheting. It had been a taxing young womanhood for her as she sacrificed to meet obligations and educate her younger siblings. For her, there was no humour in the past. Her silent recrimination was always a damper on family reunions.

My grandfather was not a keen participant either. He roamed the fields, climbed the hilltops and came home at sunset, then disappeared into his room after the evening meal and prayers. As soon as he left the room my grandmother would look up from her lap and nod her head like a bird at each sentence spoken by any of her children. Kenneth and Clara, the youngest, were the loudest.

As if to goad my grandfather, Uncle Kenny liked to recount the story of the Pedi women refusers. They rejected my grandfather's zeal to convert them and would not come to his school. One day, when they were decked out in their best to attend an initiation ceremony, he rushed at them to fulminate about their heathenism. In the fashion of burlesque dancers, they turned around in unison and lifted their beaded minis, showing him their naked backsides.

Throughout my childhood this was a story that was keenly repeated, and with each telling my aunts and uncles laughed until tears rolled down their cheeks, until they blew their noses on their handkerchiefs, until the room got eerily silent for a moment and the legendary angel passed by, causing one of them to sigh aloud as a signal to change the subject. Those were the best times of our lives, when there was a choice of laps on which you could nestle and wake up in the morning not remembering how you got into bed.

We were loved for no reason but that we were alive and bore in our features reminders of others loved before. We were easy to love as we had not yet learnt to disagree.

I do not remember much being said about my grandmother's family except that she had been a Miss Ramokgopa. Had Ouma known the drama of my paternal grandparents' marriage, I am sure she would have told me. It is only lately, after returning from exile, that I appreciate her courage: to marry a man who was not only a Christian but did not originate from her own clan. It was a daring act for a woman of her time. Her mother died when she was born and she was saved from death by one of her uncles. It was the custom then to bury the newborn baby with the dead mother but one of her uncles found her a foster mother who raised her. He betrothed her, at marriageable age, to a wealthy old man whom she did not love. She ran away to a nearby Christian community, from which she had to flee when her family sent a search party to forcibly return her to her old husband. This time she fled to a Lutheran mission station in Nylstroom where the Franz family, who headed the Lutheran mission, took her in. She became their household servant and converted to Christianity. She was the daughter of a royal Ramokgopa family, which made the story of her birth, her betrothal, her flight and her conversion legendary. My grandfather, a teacher and a Lutheran himself, sought her out, courted her and married her. They had a nomadic life, moving several times in the Pietersburg area until they settled down in Randjesfontein, where my grandfather set up the Masekela School and where his eldest children taught when they qualified. They had six children together and all were well educated, taking turns to ensure their younger siblings got a good education.

Kenneth William Dunbar Masekela was their last child. She called him Willie.

Kenneth was highly unconventional and loud about his opinions, and did not mince his words about what he called the hypocrisy of the Christian religion. Not averse to imposing corporal punishment himself, he never tired of revisiting the cruelties of his own childhood labour on the family farms

where he was raised. He poked fun at the past and was determined to build his own world where he would always have the
last word on how to run his life. He was jovial, hardworking and
generous to a fault, and in his lifetime he built schools, educated
university students and did not see any reason why he should
direct his wealth to his immediate family only. He worked hard
at creating that wealth, rising at dawn to attend to every detail
of his business. He loved serving his customers personally and
was always at the cash register in the evenings, chatting with
the buyers, asking them in broken isiNdebele about members
of their family. His enquiries about their offspring were always
about their progress. Typically, they were youth whom he had
tried to help through school. He took a vicarious pleasure in
the educational journeys of the youth and never tired of stim-
ulating their imagination for something different and new. He
never set foot in a church except for funerals of family and
close friends, and for his own four weddings, which all ended
in divorce. He was greatly amused by and amusing about the
sermons and the mien of churchgoers.

In 1978, after not seeing Hugh for eighteen years, and ten
years after visiting me in Zambia, my mother came to America
to visit us in New York and Los Angeles. On her return via
Monrovia to see my son Mabusha and my niece Pula she found
Kenneth dead and buried. She was to die three months later.

Kenneth had written to me in New York a few months earlier,
asking if he could come and visit me. He said that he needed to
see me and explain why he had said some of the things he'd had
no business saying to me. He needed my forgiveness, he said. I was
living in New York, commuting to my teaching job at Livingston
College, Rutgers University. Hugh was living in Los Angeles, but
mostly on the road, and Mabusha was in Guinea with Miriam
Makeba. Hugh and I both made feverish preparations for his visit,

which we planned with great excitement. About a week before his arrival a letter came, saying he was no longer coming and that the whole idea of his visit had not been properly thought through.

He was murdered in KwaThema, Springs, where he had lived since his expulsion from Kilnerton. He was alone in his shop late at night. It was a gruesome assault carried out with knives and axes. There were pieces of him all over the shop. He had fought back, to the death. There was no evidence of a robbery. It was a premeditated attack carried out with intent to kill. He had always been a non-conformist, forging his lifetime path with self-made wealth. It granted him the freedom to live his life according to his own precepts and seeking no counsel from anyone. He told me once when I was eighteen years old how his ambition in life was to do something that would make our little world shudder. It would be an action that broke all the rules and silenced the hypocrisy and phony demeanour of the so-called up-and-coming middle class.

My uncles Kenneth and Bigvai were our little fathers by custom. Without fail, we were taught that our first cousins were our siblings. The family programme included compulsory visits to one another to ensure the continuity of our family bonds, irrespective of whichever strains and stresses occurred in the relations of the elders. In the same way, my father's sisters (*bo Rakgadi*) Clara Xaba and Johanna Lekgetha always maintained a warm relationship with us, writing us letters and bringing us presents when they came to visit their parents.

My grandparents were shuttled between the homes of their sons on extended visits, after the government declared their home in Walmansthal a black spot. In a move to snuff out all recriminations arising out of the constant back-and-forth between residences, Uncle Kenny built a cottage for his parents on his property in KwaThema. In typical fashion, he set up strict regulations regarding when they could come into his house and how to behave in his domain – which, of course, extended beyond his own home.

A major restriction was that they would have to temper their need for interaction with the neighbours with greater discretion. They were expected to refrain from sharing details about his household affairs, no matter how innocent. Now this proved to be a difficult hurdle since privacy is not a hallmark of township life, where the space is limited and everyone is privy to one another's movements. The neighbours watch you come and go, they can tell what you are having for dinner from smelling the cooking on your stove, they know your musical preferences and your raised voice. They can judge your lifestyle from the laundry on the line and hear your children cry. Besides, greetings over the fence naturally lead to an exchange of some confidences, from your own health to the latest apartheid legislation.

As the wife of the local Lutheran evangelist and a door-to-door vendor of eggs and chickens, my grandmother had maintained her family and her sanity from the social intercourse she cultivated trudging the dusty rural roads. Her customers quenched her thirst and she could rest in the shade for a moment and catch up on the local news, away from her stern, Bible-bashing husband. She had carved a way of life for herself and it gave her a portion of freedom that she kept to herself and which made up for the lonely life on the isolated mission farm where her husband was always in the fields. He had chosen the solitary spiritual life but my gregarious grandmother – a princess in the Ramokgopa clan of the Batlokwa, and much younger than her husband – was an enterprising, outgoing woman who found her niche selling eggs to ensure the education of her children. They were grateful that their youngest son had taken them in, but chafed under his strict regime.

Kenneth was more like his father than he cared to admit, and very unlike his older brothers. My softly spoken Uncle Bigvai, after whom I named my eldest son, Mabusha, proved to be the most courageous of them all. Although he had been a founder of the African National Congress Youth League with Mandela and Sisulu, he was part of the breakaway group led by Mda and Sobukwe, to form the Pan Africanist Congress. He was the gentle one among his siblings. But in the end, his role in politics led to his imprisonment and subsequent death. As a diabetic, his bad health was exacerbated by his jailers' deliberate refusal to ensure his access to essential medicines and medical attention.

His family could not have been at ease with his political activism. Much as they had all chosen to engage in careers that would uplift the social status of the communities they lived in, they tended to avoid the political risk that would unhinge the stability that most in their class pursued quietly. They eschewed the mannerisms of social climbers and in their modest lives were content to do as much as possible to improve the lives of those among whom they lived. The deeply ingrained values of service learnt from their missionary background were enduring; as individuals, they were convinced that their actions could have ripple effects. Bigvai, like very few others of his background, had made the dangerous choice of challenging the apartheid government.

IN ALEXANDRA I learnt that as a girl I could be abducted (*skepped*) by any lout surveying the streets from a corner that was his only kingdom. Sex education was mainly about menstruation, when girls had to be warned to keep away from boys to avoid the disgrace of pregnancy before marriage. Good girls preserved their virginity until marriage and virtue was enforced only through severe restrictions on movement. Although pregnancy outside of marriage was frowned upon, children born out of wedlock were commonly embraced as part of the family. But in law they were labelled as illegitimate.

My own sex education was gained through secretly reading the sex manual that was hidden in my parents' bedside table drawer. For weeks I rushed from school straight into their bedroom to read about coitus while I was pretending to sweep and dust and tidy. At fourteen I had not yet menstruated but had already seen the blood-blotted underwear that my mother would soak in cold water at night. She would rise at dawn to wash the offending laundry before we all got up. But everything was hush-hush, so we had to pick up half-baked information from wherever we could.

One of the most discomfiting experiences for me was seeing the movie *Samson and Delilah* with my parents at the Plaza Bioscope in Alex. There were no overt scenes of sexual activity in the film, but there was an implicit lewdness in Delilah's boldness and revealing attire. She had the power of a temptress who could make a man do her bidding. I was uneasy watching her alluring movements, and it did not help that some of the audience, especially young boys who had already seen the film, were making lewd remarks, warning Samson not to catch the bait. I sat quietly between my parents, rigid with discomfort. This was different from going to concerts and ballroom dances at the Bantu Men's Social Centre, where everyone behaved with a practised decorum firmly set down by the doyennes of the township elite. We never went back to the Plaza cinema together again. Perhaps more than anything else my parents realised that they could not protect me from the realities of township life, regardless of their status.

Soon, my day came. There was a youth called Ntambo who hung around on the street corner with his gang, on 12th Avenue, where we lived. He was notorious for stabbing those who crossed him and he had no respect for young or old. He had been seen forcing a passing old woman to dig deep into her bosom and hand over the knotted handkerchief that she used as her purse. I was the child of the Health Inspector so many recognised me on the street, and our resident tsotsis did not interfere with me. One day on my way home from school Ntambo accosted me. First he whistled and gestured for me to approach him. Trembling with fear I quickened my step, thinking I could ignore him. He rushed me, pulling my arm and scattering my books. Deliberately he began to twist my arm, as was then the street courting habit (*ukuplita*), also popularly known as *ukufosta*. Forcing. In fright and panic I tearfully agreed to be his *cherrie*, as girlfriends were called. Then he ordered me to meet with him on the following Friday afternoon, when he would *skep* me and we could prove our love. Dishevelled and terror-stricken, I picked up my books. There was not an adult in sight and even if there had been, no right-thinking person would have come to my rescue as his sidekicks were watching.

This version of courtship featured nothing of the romance that I had read about in my mother's English magazines, like *Woman's Weekly*. It was coercion bristling with the threat of force and violence. I rushed home, where I removed all the signs of the encounter from myself. I felt guilt and anxiety for the next few days as Friday approached. When I walked home from school for the next few days he would be there to remind me that we had an assignation on Friday. More and more frightened at the prospect of being bedded, I did not know how to broach the subject of sex with my parents.

On the appointed day I broke down crying in the morning, fearful and realising that my only way out was to tell my parents. My father was infuriated when I haltingly spilled out the news. He grabbed my hand, leading me out of the door. We walked to the corner near the Alexandra terminus. Ntambo and his gang were not there. With him still holding my hand, we went in the direction of the bus terminus to search for him. It was here that the tsotsis also preyed on working men coming home with their wages, robbing them and often wantonly stabbing them. My father went into the Chinaman's shop on the side of the street from where he could see clearly into the square. 'Go ahead,' he croaked, 'and I will follow. Don't be afraid.'

My heart was beating fast and I walked ahead, wooden with fear. As soon as he saw me, Ntambo walked towards me, dipping his knees in the famed street walk of the tsotsis. In a flash Papa rushed onto the scene and grabbed him by the scruff of his neck. Ntambo pulled out a knife but Papa deflected it with a kick and slapped him down to the ground. Unaccustomed to a challenge, two of his gang came running to join the fight. My father made short shrift of the three, banging their heads together. It was easy because Papa was a big, tall man and they were puny, malnourished youths, red-eyed from smoking dagga, full of bravado but unable to match his strength. They lay on the dusty ground whimpering as he warned them to stay away from me or be ready to die at his hands. It was a swift and scary encounter. My father took my hand and he never once looked back at the crowd that was gathering to watch the spectacle.

My days in Alexandra were numbered from then on. I had broken the street code but it also probably became one of the reasons for my mother to convince Papa that I should go to City and Suburban Coloured School in Johannesburg.

✤ ✤ ✤

IN 1954 the new fashion in Alexandra was red berets, which most girls wore at a slant. The more my parents insisted that

I did not have to do everything my township peers did, the more I fought back to be part of the vogue. Eventually I won and became the proud owner of a red beret. Still, I was not allowed to wear it to school. So, I would hide in the hedge leading to the front gate, then stuff it between my school books on my way out.

We did not have school bags then, and the size of the pile of books one could balance in the crook of the arm was in itself a badge of pride as we walked to school, alert to the dangers of the street we shared with good working people on their way to work and their everyday errands and, at times, well-dressed gangsters driving fancy cars to match their carefully coordinated American clothes. We listened to popular American songs on the radio and the gramophone, and while we knew of Joe Louis, Lena Horne, Louis Armstrong and Jesse White, we were hardly fluent in the grammar of their history. In those days, when there was no social media, we read newspapers and wrote letters, we recognised our likeness to American blacks and we were fascinated by those who were then called Negroes. Joe Louis, the famous boxer, was a hero and there wasn't a boy in the townships who did not want to be like him. Just as we knew little about our grandmothers and those before them, so we never delved into the history of slavery. We were attracted to the style and sophistication of American blacks, to their urbanity and winning performance in the arts and sports. There was very little else that was transmitted to us but the American dream, which we pursued with fervour and little questioning.

Sybil, my youngest sister, was still a baby and Mama had just returned to work after weaning her from the breast after nine months, like she had done with all of us.

My tongue had loosened and my lisp was almost gone. I could always confide in Mama, and in a household with her in-laws, Ouma and my burdened father, we confided in each other. I was learning how to speak Setlokwa, which was the only language Koko Mamoshaba could speak. Although my grandfather could read and write English and Afrikaans, he always insisted on speaking Setlokwa to us children and Afrikaans to my mother. Now sickly and old, he sat under the backyard peach tree and read his Bible and occasionally shuffled to the bedroom to lie down on the bed alone. The three grandparents called each other Mokgotsi and had three-way conversations in which Koko was on the sidelines, with everyone translating for her. There were too many of us in the small home and increasingly my father would come home late, when the old people were already in bed. Sometimes in the morning his food would still be covered with another plate on a pot of water on the side of the coal stove. My mother worked hard at being a dutiful wife and our evenings with her were always about the happy days in Payneville and City Deep.

In KwaGuqa we had lavatories in the backyard, but they were water closets. When you came back into the house they always asked, 'Did you pull the chain?' The indignity of the bucket system in Alexandra was something Mama could not live down, especially when we had visitors, mostly relatives who owned their own houses in Lady Selborne, Atteridgeville and the East Rand. It was mostly my father's relatives, who were well educated and held responsible jobs. They were the Kwakwas, Mokgokongs, Mongalos, Nakenes, all from Polokwane, which my father proudly called the Great North.

My father was at his happiest when we visited them, and all of them revelled in telling stories of their youthful days. These were his successful Batlokwa kinsmen and women, the exceptional achievers who had managed, through their pursuit of education, to represent the South African version of the 'talented tenth' that the great African American scholar W.E.B. Du Bois extolled in *The Souls of Black Folk*. We too were taught with few tools in dark classrooms with blackboards and chalk and lying history books that shamed us, calling our ancient forebears stock thieves and squatters.

My mother, with her social work diploma, was very comfortable in my father's milieu and she was able to switch between the traditional *makoti* who was fluent in Setlokwa and the woman who was not shy to debate current issues, albeit with the winning tact expected of an outsider. When we were alone with her it was easy because she had the gift of making each one of us feel as though we were the favourite child. But when we heard the car door bang at the back, the bantering and laughter ceased and we put on different faces, rushing around trying to be at attention to meet Papa's needs. Ouma always adjusted her *doek* before he entered the house. It was her special rule that he should never see her head uncovered. She observed this custom strictly. When we playfully managed to hide her *doek* she would rush into the room she shared with Koko and Ntatemogolo to cover her head before she greeted him. She was clearly chafing from living in ''n ander man se huis' (another man's house).

As her business selling fish and chips and *magwinya* started to fail, Johanna began to murmur more frequently about finding her own place to live. 'I have always been my own boss. I can't stay in another man's house in my last days.' So, she started to look for – and found – an acre of land to build on in Grasmere, a coloured township thirty-eight miles from Johannesburg, where there was still freehold for coloureds. My father drew up the plans for the two-bedroomed house with an indoor bathroom and toilet and kitchen, and a living room and sitting room combined. The rooms were spacious and there were two verandas, at the back and the front of the house. All the expenses for materials and construction were from her own savings, which she had kept at the post office since her Witbank days.

We knew that she had paid for my mother's education at Jan Hofmeyr because she made a point of mentioning it, like someone who had to justify her presence in my father's house. Now she was going, leaving Alexandra to be her own boss under her own roof. We had left KwaGuqa because the old location was to be razed and new houses built according to apartheid standards. Already construction had begun on Lynnville, a new township where there would be no ownership of land or houses by blacks. For this daughter of the Ndzundza Ndebeles who often reminisced about the milk and honey on the endless tracts of land that her grandfather had once owned, it was too much to have to move into a four-roomed box, with no land surrounding it, that she would never own. It made no difference to her that the lavatories would be inside the house – in fact, she could not imagine how anyone already living cheek by jowl with strange neighbours could then be expected to go into a room with thin walls and have a proper shit.

But I had also overheard the whispered conversations between her and my visiting mother, about the anger and the quarrels and the looming violence inside and outside her home. Having lost her only son, Khalo, she wanted to be near her daughter and safeguard her life. Ouma swore that while she had the strength to work she had to go there and help her daughter with all the housework, which included maintaining a professional life and looking after her aged in-laws. 'These two hands and these two feet have raised her to be an educated lady. She cannot be a slave while I breathe,' she would tell me after Mama's visits. 'If after all these years he wants to take you away from me then Jwana must be part of that package,' she vowed. That is why we went to Alexandra.

My imagined idyll living with my two parents was to be transmogrified. Like many African children of my era, I was thrust into a new theatre where I had to play unpractised roles with a well-taught handiness that I had gleaned from Ouma. It was a time when my parents frequently purchased the *Rand Daily Mail* and, on Sundays, *The Bantu World*. From their discussions about the news I was becoming aware that my parents were anxious about our future. In this climate I became a go-between among all parties. I translated, interpreted and anticipated, and in the process became the envoy without a mandate. I was acutely aware of my mother's predicament as a housewife, a daughter-in-law, a daughter, a mother, a social activist and a professional woman. She was thirty-nine years old and weighed down with expectations from all of us. Neighbours, some of whom were my mother's former clients at Entokozweni, came for advice about the stringent pass laws. They were being harassed to leave Johannesburg and return to where they had been born. They came to seek advice, or sometimes just plain solace. In addition, after the housework she would write reports on her numbered cases, mostly children who needed to be found foster homes or parents. My parents were reduced to interpreting the harsh new laws for them.

Frequently she would bring home a child to stay with us because there was nowhere else for him or her to go when the workday ended. It was not unusual that, when they departed, their ragged clothes washed and ironed and in a brown paper bag, they would be wearing some of Minkie's clothes or some of mine. My father never showed resentment towards these children, and my parents followed up on what was referred to as their rehabilitation. It was not unusual for us to visit them on weekends at the Talitha Home for Non-European Girls in Coronationville.

There were even fewer places of protection for needy children and young adults then than there are today, places where they could receive counselling and assistance to change their lives. Social welfare homes were mostly organised as charities. Indeed, most social facilities were punitive and they were run by charitable organisations organised by liberal white women academics in sociology, members of church-based groups, and the wives of prominent men heading public and social institutions. In particular, experienced African social workers were supervised by young, university-trained white women with no experience in the field, albeit with a strong theoretical base. There were few African professionals who did not fall under white supervision, whether liberal or apartheid.

I learnt a lot about work politics from my parents, who now seemed to converse only about work and politics. In a way, for Papa it was a continuation of his role as the son of a Lutheran evangelist. For Mama it epitomised her calling as a social worker and a woman who was intent on being all things to all people.

My parents relished their role in assisting others and they worked hard to build a humanitarian society in their chosen way that was available to them at the time. Now and again, this priority in their lives was materially at the expense of their own family responsibility, and it caused huge fissures in our homelife. But I still admire their tenacity in believing that they could help us build a wholesome and meaningful life. Indeed, they were better placed than most parents, whose efforts were marred by the demands of making a living, leaving at dawn and coming home after nightfall, tired after waiting in long queues to catch the bus back home to walk the dangerous streets of the dark city. But we had fun, practising wedding songs in the street after supper – 'Fiyela, fiyela ngoanyana,' we sang, advising the would-be bride of the menial responsibilities of marriage – going to after-school play groups at Entokozweni, listening to my parents having discussions about the problems of urban life or simply telling stories about those who had left the country, and watching live dramas like stabbings, fights and traditional Pedi or Tsonga dancers in their colourful costumes on their way to their special derbies from the veranda at number 96 12th Avenue. Best of all were the field bands, who strutted the dust in their quasi-military uniforms. Throngs of children trooped after them, walking in step with them and shouting '*Chisa!*' And I would listen once more to my parents' discussions about the latest news in the papers. The English language rolled from their tongues with wit and anxiety about the worsening fate of Africans in the future. It was the one thing about which they concurred.

More and more as I grew older, I spent time at home and my parents continued to devise family activities that kept us inside our yard. My mother had a golden voice and for a while, before I went to Inanda, in the evenings we would learn African choral songs from the tonic sol-fa music sheets that Papa had purchased from Juta bookstore. I sang alto, Mama soprano and Papa tenor. When Hugh came for the holidays from St Peter's he would make us a quartet and the house would ring with joyful sound and rare family harmony. The songs by famous South African composers were in Sesotho, isiXhosa and isiZulu, and my favourite one was 'Duda Nonkala'. It was a humorous song about the gathering of animals to celebrate the wedding of a frog.

One day Papa came home with an ancient black Wolseley car. He had been secretly taking driving lessons and we were all surprised when we saw him in the driving seat, calmly hooting at the side gate. From that day onwards, if it was still daylight the hooting became the signal for one of us children to run and open the gate for him. Mama never opened the gate for him. She was not happy that he had not bought a newer car. But she was eager to take driving lessons and Papa was to be her tutor. Several African women like Sis Vuyiswa Nokwe, whose husband was a celebrated advocate and prominent ANC leader, had appeared in *The Bantu World* for obtaining driver's licences. They were the first black women in the country to drive. In fact, Mrs Nokwe was a prominent mathematics scholar in her own right, although in her country's view she, together with other black women of her ilk, was viewed solely in terms of being the spouse of an up-and-coming African man.

My father, a very poor driver, became Mama's first driving instructor. Typically, he made drawings of the different parts of the engine to explain its mechanics and lectured Mama every evening about the steering wheel and how it worked with other parts of the mechanism. The driving lessons were short-lived – they quarrelled so bitterly that for days the lessons were abandoned because Mama would not speak to him. After several occasions of marching out of the car and threatening to walk home, it was decided that she would attend a formal driving school.

My father was always giving away money he did not have or buying art books he could not afford. Mama would only hear of his generosity when she was thanked by his grateful recipients or when, unable to suppress his excitement, he would burst into the house with his booty cradled in his arms. It was through his indulgence in books on Picasso, Henry Moore, Giacometti and Salvador Dali that I first began to appreciate the importance of artistic creativity. It helped me to understand his obsession with wood carving and sculpture. He also purchased books on indigenous African art from the continent and was at pains to explain the beauty of African masks and other artefacts to us.

Minkie and I, in our mature lives, always marvelled at how consistently our parents injected the love of beauty into us. My mother, ten years younger than her husband and married to him against her mother's will, took to his love for creativity and together they succeeded in giving us a perspective that would always be an alternative to the narrow, subjective reality of racism, paternalism and victimhood. They fashioned for us the tools to see ourselves in a universe where achievement was not dictated by race or class. There was no entitlement, only the possibility of creating our own. As the memories tumble out, I am awed by my parents' audacity and by their deep faith in our potential. We were taught that, being Masekelas, we were not better than others, but nonetheless could make a difference and hold up the family name, not least in service to others. One of my favourite lyrics is from the song 'God bless the child that's got his own'. It was written by Billie Holiday and Arthur Herzog Jr in 1939. It extols self-reliance and when I was in exile I listened to it repeatedly, encouraging myself to rely on myself.

My home was lived-in, unencumbered by shiny surfaces and gleaming floors. We had dusty piles of old books, their pages underlined and annotated with commentary in the margins. There was always a vase of flowers on the table. Papa picked and arranged the flowers. In his garden he favoured tall, seasonal species that needed special cultivation, and their names fell from his lips, belying his own surprise at knowing them. My father relished novelty in nature and in art. All his life he sought to convey his own excitement about the rewards of a searching mind and the absolute necessity of observing and recognising rarity. He lived in his own world, where he derived a joy that could not be tarnished by the expectations of others.

I do not know whether he knew that others, including his own family, saw him in a humorous light. I just know that he would mock himself yet not diminish anyone else. Gladioli, chincher-inchees, chrysanthemums, red-hot pokers he would intone, for each one giving its Latin name. He never cultivated roses. He was always surprising us with a new species of an indigenous flower from the bounty of his solitary break-of-dawn ventures into the veld. None of the red-hot pokers I see today can ever match the brilliance and the bloody cheek of Papa's. They glowed in defiance of the dusty Alexandra street, announcing to those who had eyes to see that beauty was not the preserve of the white and the wealthy. Young and old passing our house would stop to admire my father's garden and ask him questions, which he was only too happy to answer with a flourish of botanical detail. Horticulture is an absorbing pastime and above all it requires keen powers of continuous observation, he told me. His favourite garb was a navy-blue overall with its trouser legs stuffed into his giant gumboots.

Both of my parents were enlightened products of a generation that was newly professional and mindful of their task to make a contribution to the upliftment of their own kind. They nurtured us in that ethos and taught us that the dignity of human beings did not necessarily derive from birth, wealth or power. In their way they were also irreverent about the fake power and authority of the new *indunas* who wore suits and ties and mimicked the ways of the *baas*. The subtle changes in the status of Africans in the 1940s due to the constraints of World War II had effected a short period of advancement, especially for skilled and semi-skilled Africans. The shortage of labour, with the enlistment of white men to fight in the war, meant that their services were better paid than before, although their wages were still lower than those of white women The latter for a time flooded the factories and government offices. When the war ended, Africans were once more thrust into conditions of uncertainty as the white men returned to claim their stake.

But history could not be stayed. Trade unionism had grown and the seed of worker rights had been sown to grow into the burgeoning movement for African liberation in South Africa. The new *indunas* earned more and carried exemptions that allowed them residence in the towns. In turn, because they could afford it, they had greater access to education for their children and their extended families. Socially they associated among themselves and married into one another's families, and in the parlance of the times they were called 'situations', presumably because of their incontinent use of that English word in their conversations. They were both the joke and pride of the townships and in some cases their copycat lifestyle alienated them from humble local folk. In a sense they were not dissimilar to what is now referred to as Model C types, whose speech and behaviour are seen as removed from those who have never left the township.

In some respects, although we lived in Alexandra and shared the inconveniences of basic amenities, we could access some opportunities, material and mental, that were not available to the average child in the township. In my home, my parents joked easily about the foibles of their colleagues at the workplace as well as those of close family members whom we saw at funerals, weddings or clan reunions that we attended as a matter of course. They were blessed with humour. We listened from the sidelines and later in life we to learnt to observe and accept the quirks of human behaviour, unencumbered by false piety.

FOUR

FREEDOM IN OUR TIME

APARTHEID WAS showing its teeth. Forced removals, prison gangs working on white farms and in public spaces, especially in the small rural towns, slavery on the potato farms, pass raids, banishments and namings trailed all over the land. But the voices of resistance, hoarse from screaming out the injustices, were also rising. And as we listened we heard of boycotts and the defiance campaigns in the unlikeliest of places.

Then the people answered with the Freedom Charter. The deafening clamour for 'freedom in our time' was in a moment eclipsed by the Treason Trial. It was my first year at Inanda when 156 leaders of the ANC and their allies were charged with treason. It was as though the guardians of the people had suddenly been taken away from them. We lived in a country where executions, especially of black convicted criminals, were a common feature. The sudden and stealthy nature of the arrests, which were effected so that they were simultaneous nationwide and carried out at the crack of dawn, was eerie. It was a sinister occurrence, a naked show of the power of the security forces over those who dared to challenge the state. This national swoop hit close to home. Among the arrested were Chief Albert Luthuli and MB Yengwa, the husband of Edith Sibisi, our most senior African teacher at Inanda. It had a huge psychological impact on the girls at school and became the moment when many of us began to consider our future role in the unfolding political sphere.

Fighting talk and peaceful resistance merged into armed struggle, giving birth to Umkhonto we Sizwe and other armed resistance groupings as the only alternative to the ever-burgeoning repression. Nelson Mandela, in a dramatic and unexpected move, subsequently left the country secretly to train as a guerrilla and to seek assistance from independent Africa. There was a swell of pride when he returned to the country and lived underground – and, for a while, eluded capture. He was dubbed the Black Pimpernel; the word 'terrorist' became commonplace as pamphlet bombs detonated in city centres, scattering leaflets calling for resistance against the apartheid regime. The presence of what were called 'subversive elements' in the face of heightened repression deepened the hope for change. No amount of mass arrests, detention or torture seemed to deter the spread of rebellion in the heart of the urban and rural areas. Change would be delayed, but it was inevitable, and it was beginning to make itself evident in the most unexpected quarters.

A few years later, Manto Mali (Manto Tshabalala), my erstwhile prefect at Inanda, was in one of the first groups to leave the country to join the liberation movement in Tanzania. Later on another Inanda girl, Joyce Sikhakhane, also made her mark in the struggle. But they are only a few of the many Inanda girls who made a lasting contribution to the cause of freedom in South Africa.

Our generation had been raised to step in whenever the breach of any convention became a threat to human dignity. So as I scrubbed, polished, baked and cooked, sometimes with Sybil on my back, I took on my mother's burdens. I did not relish the work – at times, I even resented it – but it always won me a special place in the hallowed universe of my mother. There were many whispers, many people disappearing to join the struggle in exile. Among them was Alfred Nzo, who had worked with my father at the Alexandra Health Committee. Another outstanding leader from Alexandra was the unforgettable Thomas Titus Nkobi, outspoken and unpretentious, without fear or bias, who became the longest-serving treasurer general of the ANC and a legend for the honest manner in which he shepherded the finances that kept the organisation afloat during the most difficult time of repression for decades in exile and at home. I was to meet many of them in Lusaka when I went to study at the University of Zambia. Their warmth and kindness towards me in exile was a validation of my parents' devotion to the service of the people of South Africa. In a world where people from different parts of the country were meeting for the first time away from home, it was heartwarming to meet men and women who knew my parents and appreciated their work.

When my sister Elaine was about eight she spoke Xitsonga, which she was learning from MaMatsheka, who had come from a Tsonga village to live with her husband, a clerk at the Alexandra Health Committee. In the townships, Tsongas were called Shangaans, and often ridiculed for their language and their rustic dress style. In particular, their love for bright primary colours was mocked and earned the scorn of township fashion icons who favoured the American sporty style or the straight British tweed. At school there was general teasing of all ethnic groups, especially those who came from the furthest parts of the old Transvaal. In the urban bustle of making a living, the narrow differences between customary origins were muting into a shared clamour for change, and the stereotyping based on tribal background was retained in the undertones of tired jokes in closed groups of intimate homeboys and homegirls who dared not to speak their bias publicly.

My mother spoke almost all the African languages, which enhanced her community work and endeared her to all. Very few called her a coloured to her face because, like many others, she had been raised to speak isiNdebele fluently. With her aptitude for languages, she also spoke isiXhosa and Sepedi without an accent. This was not a remarkable skill because she had been raised in an African environment, as had many of her background, born before apartheid. But in an increasingly racially defined society it would become the norm that people of her background would eschew any commonality with Africans, choosing Afrikaans and English as their only languages. My mother blended easily into all the communities she lived in, although there were rare occasions when there were murmurs about her background and racial epithets were deliberately expressed loudly enough to be heard.

Whereas in the past the word 'coloured' had been used loosely to describe people of mixed heritage, now, with Verwoerd as the Minister of Native Affairs, racial classification was becoming the norm. Certain privileges in pay, residence, education and pensions placed coloureds in a separate category. Crude tests like running a pencil through the hair were used to determine one's status. In fact, there were many men and women of mixed heritage in the townships and villages who could have passed for white but did not speak a word of English or Afrikaans, and continued their lives untouched by the new legislation. But especially in the established urban areas, there were those who were at pains to be reclassified, and many acquired their new identity with zeal, rejecting their kinship to Africans.

It is still a mystery to me how we came to be Afrikaans-speaking, because Walter Bower was supposedly Scottish and from Natal. Of course, a great number of Ndebeles from the Eastern Transvaal spoke Afrikaans because Dutch was the medium

of instruction at the Lutheran bible schools. But there was Ouma
Sussie, who spoke perfect Dutch, yet in her home isiNdebele was
the mother tongue. And her and Ouma's mother, Ouma Kappie,
all outfitted in long, traditional, black Dutch clothing, including
the *kappie*, never ever to my memory uttered a word of Dutch.
I can only suppose that somewhere along the line, somehow,
Ouma decided that she, too, like her rival in Doornfontein,
would raise her children to be Afrikaans-speaking. It was common among certain groups raised in areas where Afrikaans was
the dominant language, such as the Transvaal and the Orange
Free State, for people like my Ouma Sussie to speak Afrikaans
with ease, without assigning it a role in their homes. But I remember how the older people spoke of other African nationalities with
a sense of wonderment. Even then it was a sign of worldliness to
have encountered Africans from outside their own closed circle
of Ndebeles. The references to amaChopi, Griquas, amaXhosa,
amaSuluman, Vhavenda and even Ethiopians were peppered with
a definite wonder about their dress, languages and diet, without
any prejudice or rejection. It was more of a fascination at discovering something new in the variety of the human species and
apprehending the distances beyond the disintegration of one's
own little world. These strangers were a comforting sign that
there was something more, beyond. The exotic propelled their
imagination beyond the strictures of their own confines and they
were untainted by prejudice. The existence of *oorlams* (accultur-
ated people) also held a measure of exoticism. Clearly African,
many spoke not a word of an indigenous language. They were
the stubborn evidence of indentureship and slavery in South
Africa, there for all to see but hardly acknowledged. Now, when
I read the new history of my country – which is still not in
the school textbooks – I am struck by the extent to which the
Eastern Transvaal was a thoroughfare for most comers in search

of their own version of a fortune, be it guns, game, diamonds, gold or coal. By then, after the conquests of the Pedis, Ndebeles and Tswanas, most of the land had been taken. Tradition dictated that the men could only get married if they had the requisite number of cattle. Since they also needed money to pay the compulsory taxes, earning it in the mines was their only option. But guns were a lucrative deal too, especially in the earlier period when they thought they could still defend their land corridor for all the nationalities of South Africa and even foreigners seeking their fortune in Southern Africa. From the point of view of the reigning Europeans, it was the Africans who were portrayed as the architects of their own poverty and the cause of all the redefined ills of the past and the present, although the avarice of the Europeans was there for all to see.

Ouma had said that she had come from the Ndzundza Ndebeles, but — already lured by the spirit of a growing urban culture that was in strong opposition to the tribal homelands policy of apartheid — I was not curious to know more about her past or that of my father's Pedi people. To most of us younger people witnessing the ravages of apartheid, progress meant rejecting the past — especially as it was being used by the regime to make us foreigners in our own land. At any rate, what we learnt formally at school was hardly an incentive. The history texts served as a paean to the heroes of colonialism and the defeat of the Africans. Sekhukhune, Sobhuza, Shaka and Moshoeshoe were mentioned in passing. They had been vanquished by the superior firepower of the Europeans. And the Khoi and San, we read, had just been nomads wandering about the desert with their poisoned arrows until their susceptibility to alcohol and smallpox had rendered them too weak to withstand civilisation, and they had died out.

In fact, it is only now that I have also learnt the roots of the *oorlams* culture, in part made up of the Khoi and San who, through the system of indenture, had become a subculture of the Afrikaans community. They were forever striving to pay for their freedom and rarely gaining it, caught in the ruthless demand for labour to benefit the ZAR farmers who had left the Cape in anger after the abolition of slavery in the colony. Now we know that in the Transvaal there were organised raids on African women and children, who were sold as slaves to Dutch households. Some managed to escape at great risk to their lives but the rest adopted the Dutch language and culture and were kept in bondage to supply the skills that the Boers needed. They regarded themselves as apart from the indigenous people in the area and married among themselves, often becoming the original urban black residents in towns. It is not far-fetched to deduce that my granny sisters could, at some stage of their troubled lives, have been indentured, that they could have been virtual slaves at a young age. Why, then, the story Ouma told of being about ten years old and running from the farm kitchen where she worked to hide in the bush to spy on a regiment of white soldiers braaiing meat? This was clearly during the so-called Second Boer War. But long before then, indigenous women and children, when they were not killed during battles, were often the booty of these marauding gangs with their indigenous *agterryers*, themselves skilled artisans who were forced labourers attending the wagons and the weaponry of the descendants of the early Voortrekkers. These indentured mechanics of their time, often of Khoisan origin, had no choice but to be the lackeys of the Boers, in war and in rare peacetime. Their expertise in steel, wood and iron was highly sought after by both powerful chiefdoms and their rival settlers.

That whole territory of the Ndzundzas was a melting pot that scotches claims of racial purity in South Africa, yet this is true of any place where Europeans and indigenous people have happened to meet. This convergence bred a new generation, marked by the diversity that is the hallmark of the new South Africa. It is living proof that culture is not a virgin that can be preserved. To a large degree, it is a proven fact that only those who have remained untouched are in isolated enclaves sealed off from the history of mankind. The Eastern Transvaal was one of the arenas of encounter between indigenous peoples and Europeans who, despite their assumptions of superiority, became the mere ingredients in the soup of a new natural mix.

The route to the diamond fields, to the gold and coal mines and the agricultural fields, stirred the greed of takers from all the cardinal points of South Africa – and of the poor working men from Europe, and as far away as America, who all grabbed whatever they could on their way to finding their fortune. The Africans who inhabited the land were mere instruments for achieving those goals, if not impediments that could be bought and sold. Yes, I did hear my granny sisters speak of Lydenburg and Waterval Boven, of King Solomon of the Zulus who was exiled there when they were young women, and Ouma, a reluctant storyteller, was sometimes so overcome by memories that she could not repress the tales that burst out of her shackled memories of the Kimberley diggings. Villains, robbers, diamond smugglers, scammers selling fake stones, African women from all parts of the country coming to make their fortune selling home-made beer to the miners, these were some of her themes. I now appreciate that black women in these new industrial hubs were considered surplus, especially in the light of the physical labour required from black men. But women like my ouma were pressed to find the means to support the children and the old whom they had left behind with relatives. They were smart women, inventing plans as they moved along in unfamiliar towns, often hearing new tongues they had to learn to speak, seeking ways to escape poverty.

Piecing together fragments of stories it is clear that Ouma followed Walter Bower to Kimberley. Whether he wanted her there we cannot confirm, but certainly he involved her in his transactions, which may or may not have included the smuggling of diamonds and the making and selling of alcohol. What is known is that she came back to KwaGuqa with enough money to build the house where she raised my mother and Uncle Khalo, the home that was the only one I had until we moved to Alexandra. Finding her own place in the semi-rural coloured township of Grasmere, now called Ennerdale, was like founding a new heritage, and she believed strongly that she would lay the basis for all of us, her descendants. It may be a crude way of putting it, but I have no doubt that in her mind she was also seeking a way to get back at those who had thwarted her forefathers, who had scattered them and their offspring like chaff, who had reduced the cycles of all her life to mere survival and petty existence, wasted dreams and bitter memories.

Some, who were rural in origin but now ensconced in coloured townships, pretended not to understand African languages, which made for great fun for me and Mama travelling on the bus to Ouma in Grasmere. There was a blue-eyed, straight-haired man with an aquiline nose who marched up and down the aisle of the moving bus, insulting the coloured passengers in perfect isiZulu.

'*Izinja!*' (Dogs!) he would shout. 'You pretend not to understand me. Yes, sit quietly as though you don't know what I speak of. Sit here like the Europeans, who think they are better than blacks. You are no better than animals who kill their own kin. You call yourselves *kleurlinge* (coloureds). What the f— is that when we all know that you are part of the African race? Some of you have not even got a primary school education but just because the comb slips through your hair and the apartheid pencil will not stay on your head, just because you earn more at the factories where you slave for crumbs from the table of the evil white man, you think you are better. On Sunday night you will be borrowing money to go to work on Monday yet you preen here with your lipsticks and your fine combs … My first lesson today is '*inja*', which means 'dog', or '*hond*' in your chosen language. Next week we will be talking about snakes and I will teach you what you already know but pretend not to understand.'

On and on he would go, stopping only to take a sip from his bottle of brandy. Their heads bowed or looking straight ahead, everyone on the bus was silent. Mama and I also sat quietly, repressing our hilarity and stealing quick looks at each other, a little nervous that he might pounce on us for support. My light-skinned mother was our passport to Grasmere and everyone knew she was married to an African. Grasmere, where Ouma now lived on her own land and in her own house.

Not in another man's house.

❖❖❖

LOWEST ON the totem pole in the hierarchy of Alexandra were the amaMpondo, whom we never saw in daylight because they were the very foundation on which Alexandra's health system was built. They carried the night soil, full buckets of human excrement, and replaced them with clean buckets. They were the only inhabitants of the township who moved without fear at night, in the streets of the Dark City.

They were feared and despised. They wore balaclavas to cover their noses for the stench, and ragged heavy overalls and gum-boots, and they brooked no interference in their work. No one dared to enter their dwelling places or cared to break their sullen routine. They did not want to be seen and we, hiding behind lace curtains and closed windows, could not imagine that they were fathers, brothers, uncles, cousins and husbands. Their voices warred with the clanging buckets and disappeared into the empty streets, muffled softer and softer by the heavy-duty trucks that sped away in the night carrying our sewage to an unknown depot.

There were rumours of an impending strike by the night-soil men, and my parents spoke softly to each other, weighing the risks my father was taking as the messenger of the Alexandra Health Committee. She was cautioning him and he was wearily explaining that it was his job to listen to their complaints. My father spoke isiXhosa and isiZulu with a heavy Sepedi accent and very bad grammar, but he could carry on a cheerful conversation with disarming aplomb. He had an affecting enthusiasm that won him attention, and no small amount of admiration, from his listeners for his eager efforts to please and to amuse.

His return, late one night, from a meeting with the night-soil men was announced by a reek that filled every room in the house. It was the custom in the house to wait until morning to hear the outcomes of his nocturnal outings. But that night, half-asleep, we heard the movements as water was boiled, the tin bath brought into the kitchen and water fetched again by my mother from the communal tap on the side wall of where we slept. By then the whole house smelled like a hospital and I could imagine the Dettol snaking into the clear water of his bath and whitening it. A bucket of night soil had been spilled on his body. The following day he went to work as though nothing had happened and the incident was never spoken of again.

It was time to move again.

By then, in steady progression, my parents had already lived in City Deep, George Goch, Benoni and Springs. From being a schoolteacher at the Masekela School in Randjesfontein, from which my parents moved to Walmansthal, to becoming a mine policeman in Witbank and thereafter a mine clerk, and then getting onto the lowest rungs of the Health Inspectorate, my father was now Chief Health Inspector of Alexandra. He had steadily increased his qualifications through correspondence schools until he had the equivalent of a university degree. Ouma had no appreciation for my father's endeavours because he had no land or house to call his own. She lamented the fact that he always lived in houses that belonged to his employers. She always pointed out that he was still obligated to her because he had never paid lobola and that it was she who had financed Mama's studies, even though she was already married to my father.

She took all the credit for my mother's high qualifications in social work. 'All of you were brought to me at nine months so your mother could pursue her brilliant career. *Dit is almal Jwana se werk.* (You are all Jwana's work.) It's only Sybil I did not raise.'

Mama was now a senior social worker at Entokozweni and an external examiner for the Jan Hofmeyr School, her alma mater. Throughout their marriage, each move signalled an improvement in their well-being and an advance in their social status. Like many of their peers in the South Africa of the time – teachers, nurses, court interpreters, priests, businessmen, farmers and a rising number of university graduates who were lawyers, lecturers and doctors – they were respected and admired for acquiring an education. By reason of laws and practices aimed at cutting Africans down to size, their professional lives were limited by their white Afrikaner supervisors, some of whom had never even seen the door of a secondary school.

My mother was a versatile woman of her times. Her favourite word was 'progressive'. As much as she wrote reports deep into the night, she paid equal attention to ironing, folding and pressing while my father studied for exams, or worked on his sculpture designs at the side of the big kitchen table. They took breaks, drinking tea and chatting to each other. My father hardly drank alcohol, unless we had male visitors. Then he would unearth the single bottle of brandy from the crowded bottom of the wardrobe of their bedroom suite with the twin beds, which were the fashion of the time. An American innovation, twin beds were popular in the townships where the houses were so small that a properly sized marriage bed could not be accommodated.

I had my first period at fifteen, away from home. My mother had stuffed sanitary pads into my luggage, mumbling that I could use them when it came and that the people at school would help me. The obligatory lecture on sex and feminine hygiene was delivered to me by the prefects at school. I fondly remember many other Inanda Seminary girls like Neo Moerane, Gugu Gcabashe, Joyce Makwakwa, Stella Alexander and Joyce Ngcobo and my teachers, Edith Sibisi and Nomthandazo Shezi. I believe that all of them walked in the Light.

IT WAS the beginning of the end of my parents' marriage. The raging subject at home was Minkie, away at St Peter's and threatening to become a musician, and shattering my parents' ambition for him to become a medical doctor. As the firstborn son he had disappointed my parents, but armed with her social work training my mother quietened her qualms about his choice of vocation and pressed for him to be allowed to follow his calling. I adored my brother and supported him. Again, I was caught up in the differing attitudes in my family and found myself a conduit to each of them. This was eased by the fact that my father was partial to me. I was brilliant in school and became his new hope: that

I would fulfil the promise of a Masekela university graduate, a BA.

Papa would call out, 'Babsie!' from the garden as I was helping my mother in the house. Smiling, Mama would wink and say, 'Go, work with your papa, Assistant in Chief. I will cope here.'

It was our unspoken promise to work together to appease my father. I fetched and carried for him as he named, in Latin, the stones, plants and soils to me. He lost himself in gardening and design. He immersed himself in the health of the goldfish, which glided and dived between the broad leaves of the water lilies, raving white in the clear waters of the pond. Cemented to the bottom of the pool were smooth pebbles of various shades, all in rounded shapes and each a different height. In there, the little fish frolicked, dodging around obstacles or simply swimming straight up to linger momentarily under the green blanket of broad leaves almost covering the surface of the pond. Beneath the small rockery blooming with red-hot pokers, aloes and other colourful water-shy plants, our little fenced garden thwarted the dusty gravel road that was 12th Avenue. It declared itself in a language that Alexandra could never become.

You could only reach the backyard by walking through the front door into the front room and straight through the kitchen. There, in a small shed, halted in their tracks, stood rows of sculptures, in various forms of supplication, their arms arching towards the heavens, every one of them in questioning anguish. They just stood there, ramrod stiff, shrouded by black plastic, powdered down with grey dust. In the phrase my father sometimes used, they were a 'forgotten factor'. He could stay away from them for months, not even glancing towards the shed as he came and went every day. They stood on watch, still and silent sentinels that spoke volumes. They held their own, rigid and unfinished, a testament to the vaccination campaigns against smallpox, polio and tuberculosis.

When my father spoke of SANTA it was not Father Christmas but the South African National Tuberculosis Association. He inspected milk and other food outlets, and supervised milk distribution and general hygiene in Alexandra. In a place where slaughtering cows, sheep, goats and chickens in the backyard was a commonplace weekend event in preparation for weddings, funerals and baptisms, he was not always popular with everyone because he stuck to regulations. It was not unusual for him to become part of the slaughtering team if it was the only way he could ensure that proper sanitation rules were followed.

Apart from his educated extended family, most of whom he described as having 'arrived', his close friends were the Chinese shopkeepers on the busy 'square' in Alexandra near the PUTCO bus terminus during his Lin Yutang days. On the bookshelf in our front room were titles like *The Importance of Living*, *With Love and Irony* and *The Gay Genius*. Although at fourteen I was ravenous about reading anything on the printed page, it was just impossible to follow the language or the thrust of these books. But I was also intrigued and awed by the fact that my father could draw pleasure from them. It placed him in another order of intellectual exercise into which I could not gain entry, and this was frustrating and estranging. It was a barrier. One I had to climb over. Next to them on the shelf were also a string of Aldous Huxley books with even more peculiar titles, such as *Eyeless in Gaza*, *Brave New World*, *The Doors of Perception* and *The Perennial Philosophy*.

I can see, now, that as political repression was heightening, when the major apartheid laws like the Group Areas Act, the Bantu Education Act and the Bantu Authorities Act were being enforced, he threw himself into a frenzy. It was far more important to him to demonstrate that Africans were capable of keeping contagious diseases at bay under the most unfavourable conditions than to wear a suit and tie and shiny shoes. There was always something of the rural man in him and, except for his wedding picture outfit, I don't remember him as a dapper man. Tall and hefty, there was always some part of his dress that was unbuckled, untied, unbuttoned or lacking in shine.

The regulation and management of the bucket system of latrines, which was the blight of Alexandra, was his most demanding task and he undertook it with an eminent team of African inspectors. Some of the colleagues on this team held BSc degrees. One of them, Alfred Nzo, became the first foreign minister in the democratic government headed by Nelson Mandela. Overcrowded and growing, the Dark City, so close to the expanding City of Johannesburg, had the Jukskei River on its northern border. Some parts of the river were already choking with pollution, and when it rained the water flooded the rickety dwellings on the banks. And this, today, is still a recurring event, unchanged by our acclaimed democracy, by our hard-fought triumph over the bigotry and the unspeakable brutality of apartheid. This fear that those shacks clinging to the edges of the abyss will topple over into the dirty water is still the same.

The dongas of our township, deep, gaping ravines in the middle of main streets, were just part of the scenery. We devised smart detours to avoid crossing them, or simply descended into the crater from one side of the street to cross the stream of dirty water at the bottom and then ascend to emerge on the other side of the street. No doubt, when he started there, my father believed that he could transform the Jukskei River into the clear waters of the rivers of his Limpopo childhood. Working full time and forever studying for another higher certificate, my father always burnt the candle late into the night, always with a lit cigarette drooping between his lips. During the summer rains, the donga shortcuts were forbidden, but it was not rare to find a dead body in the morning, drowned by impatience, drunkenness or crime.

Typically, my father's language about his work was peppered with Latin terms that named the rocks, the rushing soil washed clean of nurture, and the unwanted growth of straggling plants that stalked the soft sides of the dongas. Papa knew the Latin name of every weed, every noxious growth and each living thing that was attached to it. Here and there would be crooked, slender saplings contending for life.

Some of the words from his mouth still echo in my own speech. Design, environment, the grain of the wood, prune, mask, sanitary, inoculate, infectious, bureaucracy, avant-garde, bohemian, emaciated. When they spring to my lips I see him, intent, self-deprecatory, mocking, one shoulder higher than the other, tall and strong, always slightly dishevelled, going into every new day with gusto.

IT WAS a difficult time in my adolescence and I was just awakening to the bright lights of Johannesburg. My brother was at St Peter's Secondary School, where the rector was Father Trevor Huddleston, whose opposition to the apartheid regime was all over the papers. Minkie was in the limelight as part of the Huddleston Jazz Band and he had my undivided support in the raging war in our home, with my father being vehemently opposed to his choice of career.

My parents' marriage was fraught with tension and silent war, and I was caught in the web of filial loyalties. Under the circumstances I translated every 'no' about how I dressed or spoke, or about my choice of friends, into a form of oppression. It was different from the kind of orphanhood I had felt in

KwaGuqa. There, I felt the innocent haze of abandonment from being torn out of a happy family photo, with an angelic mother, a handsome father and an older brother who was the apple of their eye. Now, in the midst of the drama, I was discovering that at close quarters my naive imaginings had been an illusion. My Uncle Kenny played no small part in teaching me that what I felt was normal. Parents are only human and have flaws, he would reiterate. Once you accept that, you are free. Frequently, I did not even like them. I did not envy my brother but I wanted what he wanted for himself. The music he was listening to, of Miriam Makeba, Dolly Rathebe, Mackay Davashe, Clifford Brown, Louis Armstrong, Ella Fitzgerald and Billie Holiday, opened up a whole world to me. And I wanted him to be in that world. We both were under duress to do what we had not chosen. He did not want to be a doctor and I did not want to go Inanda. We both knew that Mama did not necessarily agree with us but that she would always support us. Hugh knew that I would never win against going to Inanda but we both understood that there was no turning back for him. Eventually, he ran away from home.

There was always a newspaper in our home and the excitement of the African independence movement was something my parents discussed in a very animated fashion. If it could happen in other colonies, surely our own fate could not be sealed forever.

My mother always spoke warmly about some of the people she had studied with at the Jan Hofmeyr School. Among them were Joshua Nkomo, who became the president of the Zimbabwe African People's Union, ZAPU. Subsequently a Mr Sibande, who was also a candidate at the school, was assigned to do his practicals under her supervision, as many others had been, like Ellen Khuzwayo, Winnie Madikizela, Manye Finca and Brigalia Bam. He tried to get her to come to the then Northern Rhodesia to work. The answer at home was no.

Although reported on in a biased manner by some, the freedom struggles on the continent resonated in my being. In a twist of adolescent wishful thinking and naivete, I took the 'Wind of Change' speech, made by Harold Macmillan and discussed with hope and enthusiasm all over the country, as a mantra for what I believed was at hand in South Africa. Never mind that it was the brutalities of the Mau Mau that were emphasised, never mind that freedom fighters were characterised as bloodthirsty, raping hordes, the spirit of *Mayibuye* prodded me, and my reaction to any injustice was so heightened that I could not but become very sensitive to any constraints on my own personal life. 'Deep, deep down,' as my brother would later chant, I believed that change was imminent in South Africa. And that it would be soon, because the very chief of the Empire, Macmillan himself, had announced it.

I resented the assumption that I was an empty vessel to be filled at Inanda, and my entry there was made with profound reluctance and a begrudging spirit. I was just another powerless young girl with no say.

I wanted to attend Madibane High School in Newclare. After a year of commuting into Johannesburg, to the City and Suburban Coloured School, I could not understand the fuss about attending another day school near home.

In mitigation of my father's unbending will, and in retrospect, I now understand his position. His identity had been threatened by his eldest daughter carrying a name that did not belong to him and that had been fractured by omitting an E and an A and adding an L. Maskell.

He could never show his black face at the school but my mother could, as a nearly white, long-haired parent. In a patriarchal society that shared many of the values of the ruling power regarding male authority, he had to face his peers as one who was under the thumb of his wife. He had won the battle of preventing her from becoming a volunteer in the Defiance Campaign, was fighting the choice of his firstborn male child to become a musician, and so he had to lose the skirmish of his daughter's identity. Coupled with this was the cauldron of apartheid, which had simmered and was now boiling over, reducing him, and all black males ('non-whites', as we were called then) to indignity. He was frustrated on all counts, unable even to follow his vocation as a sculptor. He could only admire the works of great artists while he slaved as a health inspector in an island of misery and futility where he had no means to change the abject poverty and disease that loomed in the Dark City – misery that was a daily metaphor for the tragedy unfolding in his country of birth.

And so I was taken to Park Station, to embark on the train to Durban, with my trunk and my provision basket packed with a roast chicken, sardines, sandwiches, Oros orange juice, scones and a pure white kitchen towel to cover it.

MY VIRGINITY and the preservation of my virtue may have been the twin prime concerns that had played a part in my father's decision to send me to Inanda, yet I was put on a train with testosterone-charged youths from all the corners of the Transvaal 'metropoli', as my brother would subsequently sing in his anthem 'Stimela'. Of all the girls with whom I had gone to school in Witbank, in Alex and at City and Suburban in Johannesburg, I represented a miniscule percentage of black schoolgirls who were able to enter high school in 1956 with their sights set on matric. A greater number went to local high schools where they were able to achieve a Junior Certificate and enter nursing schools or teacher training colleges. A handful went on to universities, but the majority ended up as factory workers, domestic servants, clerks and unwed mothers who toiled all their lives to raise the next generation of South Africans.

Once the train left Park Station it was a free-for-all, with only the toughest surviving. It was another experience for me, of naked violence against females. Boys roamed the corridors of the moving doors shouting out the names of girls, banging on the sliding doors of the compartments, threatening to break down the doors. Shaking with fear, we cowered in the dark, crowded train cars, hoping for the appearance of the Afrikaner conductors to save us. But they only came in the morning, sneering as they snatched our tickets.

This was very different from my first trip to Durban as a child, with Hugh and me wearing labels around our necks to identify us. Later, when I was twelve, we drove for twelve hours by car with my parents and Ouma. Almost sixty years old then, she had never seen the sea. She vowed to her God that she was ready to join Him after she had seen this wonder of His immaculate creation.

What was the same was Auntie Clara waiting at the platform to meet me and escort me to the bus to Inanda. She left me in the care of Joyce Lindiwe Ngcobo, who became one of my 'mummies'. Her father was a lecturer at the University of Fort Hare, having obtained an MA in Economics from Yale University. Lindiwe had no airs about her background nor aims to walk the same path as her father. She was entirely relaxed in her physical beauty and applied her make-up with such great expertise that only the meanest teacher could detect it. It was her last year at Inanda and she was enthusiastic about studying nursing the following year. She once showed me a letter that her father had written to her. Enclosed in the envelope was what had inspired his response. It was her letter, underlined with grammar corrections and comments in red ink, and suggestions for improvement. It did not seem to bother her at all.

'That is Daddy's way,' she said.

To me, Lindiwe was the epitome of cool, and forever after I have always wished I could be as laid-back as she was. Later on, when we were both in exile, she lived with her husband in Canada, where she was a respected nursing professional. In all the photographs I saw of her, she looked elegant and worldly.

The two-hour trip from Durban to Inanda seemed eternal as we moved away from the city into a dense rural landscape. Unlike the open bushland of the Transvaal, where you could see for miles ahead, here the thickset vegetation on both sides of the narrow, untarred road offered barely a suggestion of human habitation. It was quiet in the bus except for an occasional hiss from the back, reminding the new girls that they were freshers, *imisila* (tails) in isiZulu. Wisely, the prefects did not bother to find the girls who made the threatening sounds. From time to time, if the hissing was too loud, one or two of them would stand up and give a severe glance towards the back. As we got closer to Inanda there were tilled lands and modest houses and the usual tableaux of waving children herding cattle and women leaning on hoes with babies on their backs. The land was hilly and there were pathways snaking between the main road and the dwellings. Now and then you would glimpse a bored dog, ears pricked, standing still and gazing into the distance as if posing for a picture. You could look deep into a general trader's shop with the owner and his family moving about inside or some messenger child emerging with a purchase wrapped in newspaper.

One of the prefects stood up to announce that we would soon be passing the Ohlange Institute, which was founded by Dr John Dube, the first president of the ANC, and which also boasted

Chief Albert Luthuli as one of its alumni. It was another world, far away from Alexandra, and I was entering it filled with dread and uncertainty. The road was bumpy and the leaves on the branches leaning into the road were thirsty, hiding their green shine underneath the dust. The conversations of the senior girls were full of musings about the women teachers we were yet to meet. They called them by nicknames. They chortled and giggled as they mimicked their voices and unsmiling faces, always searching for a broken rule. Perhaps recalling their own recent encounters, they wondered speculatively about the missionaries' wooden bodies and how interestingly a live prod would affect them. We, the new girls, sat very still, none daring to react. The prospect of becoming a senior girl beckoned and I was set on my new path.

On the Highveld the air was thin and dry. This thick, dank air was like being forced to sweat under a blanket, inhaling hot, medicated air to clear a fever. At last we were now near the seminary – there it was, the silent driveway onto the campus, bounded by tall trees on both sides. A shade was formed in the meeting of the treetops to form a canopy closing over us, and then, there, waiting, was the welcoming party made up of the principal and the teachers, in the open space near the big tree from which you could see the buildings standing at attention. Some of the girls had already arrived in earlier buses or in vehicles organised from other venues. We were mostly from the station, many of us still traumatised from the overnight train ride.

In my head, I was already composing the letter I was going to write to my parents. Of necessity the letter would be bland and formal. It would say what was expected of me and drip with platitudes borrowed from the letter-writing exercises in Standard 6. All our letters at Inanda were submitted open, with a stamp and envelope. They were then read in the principal's office by a missionary on duty or an African staff member if they were in isiZulu or another African language. At any rate, we were encouraged to write in English, just as it was compulsory to speak English only, from Monday to Friday, a rule that was broken with regularity and which caused us to be 'marked' regularly. As punishment we did physical work in the garden, hoeing for one hour per mark on Saturdays. The big subterfuge was smuggling sealed letters to willing visitors who would post them for us without the knowledge of our keepers. It was regarded as a cardinal infraction of the school rules but for us it was an opportunity to express our true feelings and especially to communicate with boyfriends. In my case, I also smuggled letters to my mother inquiring about family matters of which I did not want the authorities to know.

There were so many rules to learn and names to memorise, of students, teachers and buildings. There were schedules, clubs, associations and school duties. From the wake-up bell at 6 a.m. to the night bell at 9 p.m. we were occupied, interrupted only by meals and prayers. We were always in groups, walking to and from the dormitories to the classrooms and to the chapel. Saturdays were for laundry and hairdressing and playing tennis, or just lounging on the green grass or at the various school clubs like the Students' Christian Association. Once a year the SCA met with students from Wentworth Medical School, where the membership of the SCA swelled in the week before the meeting with the Inanda girls – just as it did at Ohlange Institute and Adams College when interschool meetings were planned. Inanda was called The Zoo by the students, especially the males, from the other nearby schools.

Local girls went home once a month for the weekend but had to be fetched and returned by adult relatives cleared by the principal's office. The veranda at the principal's office was busy on Saturday and Sunday afternoons when we were allowed outside visitors, but the protocols were very strict. Whether it was a parent you had not seen for months or a favourite uncle or aunt, you were not allowed to acknowledge a visitor until you had been cleared in the office. Until I left Inanda in 1960 I could not understand why we were expected to stiffen our necks and pretend we did not know the expected visitor, walk past them, enter the office, answer some questions and then calmly walk towards them as impassively as possible. In most cases parental approval had to be secured for a visit from a non-relative. One of my friends at Inanda, Thuladu Hlatshwayo, was well connected with the Gumede family in the village, and towards the end of my first year I met Johnny Makatini, a recent graduate from the University of Natal. He recruited me to the ANC when I was sixteen and in all the years in exile he always looked me up to make sure I remained involved in the struggle. My other visitor, who came with a friend in tow, was my cousin Ephraim Mokgokong, who was then studying medicine at Wentworth with no thoughts of one day becoming the vice chancellor of the Medical University of South Africa, Medunsa. Buti Eph is still my favourite cousin and I am glad that I did not follow his advice to become a nurse when I gained my Junior Certificate and to marry his doctor friend.

We had many eminent visitors at Inanda. One of them was Dr Alan Taylor, the head of McCord Hospital. He had a daughter who was about sixteen, and when the family came for a weekend she wore shorts and earrings, which were forbidden for Inanda girls. Our principal, Dr Scott, almost revered Dr Taylor and he was respected as much by many in the Durban community for the excellent manner in which he ran McCord and for advocating for the admission of Africans into the University of Natal Medical School. Dr Taylor was also a great friend of Albert Luthuli, and identified strongly with the anti-apartheid cause.

Once a year he was invited to give a sermon at our Sunday

morning service. When he came to preach, towards the end of my second year at Inanda, one of the African teachers also invited her new husband for the weekend. In the announcement of the names of the visitors for the weekend, I thought maybe I had misheard his name. That Friday evening, at prayers, I kept my eyes fixed on the entering visitors and there he was, walking to the front row next to Miss X, now his wife. He did not see me. I knew him from Alexandra. He had been a junior health inspector and lived in rooms in the yard we all shared through the Alexandra Health Committee. For months, he and my aunt had conducted a secret liaison until my father caught them 'red-handed', as the popular saying went. Now he was married to one of my teachers. He had discarded his Jo'burg-American style of dressing in informal colourful separates. Instead, he was now grey-suited and white-shirted and his hands were folded on his lap.

I watched him throughout the evening prayers. He had not seen me yet. The following evening we were to entertain the visitors at a special variety concert, which would include dramatic sketches, Isicathamiya, poetry and traditional dancing. I was in the school choir, and I was to sing a song called 'Where'er You Walk' by George Frideric Handel, to the accompaniment of my piano teacher, Miss Manana Cheyney. The die was cast.

As I climbed the stairs to the stage on Saturday evening I almost tripped, and I saw his moment of recognition and how he unclasped his hands as if to adjust to a more comfortable position on his seat as a slight paroxysm made him nod sharply. I remembered how my aunt had sobbed, denying that she had stalked him. I saw how he had his eyes trained on me and I marvelled at how much power I had over him at that moment as I went to take my place on the stage, next to the piano. Here, he had to be solemn and display all the outward virtues of an upright Christian man. He was so adept at playing the innocent.

I walked back to my seat after the performance, ready to enjoy the other acts. The favourite ensemble was the Isicathamiya group. Their male attire of black trousers and tuxedo jackets and white shirts and top hats drew hoots of laughter and applause, even before they started singing. Their imitation of men was hilarious precisely because there was nothing male about them but that they had focused on capturing the vanity of first-time urban dwellers with great panache. The mixture of town and country. The assembled Inanda girls screamed, shrieked and laughed helplessly as the 'men' shuffled onto the stage. They began their performance with a soft hum, their mooing heads in the shape of the crescent of the moon.

There among them was a deep bass voice, but we could not tell who its owner was. Then they started to move, dancing in unison and singing their hearts out a capella, stamping the ground soundlessly just as though they were dancing barefoot on the grass. We loved it when the bass covered the other voices, but it was the jumping in the air, the arm gestures of informal interpreters begging, understanding, that had us forgetting we were young Christian maidens who must uphold the decorum of genteel self-control. A prefect or two would rise and sweep a warning look over us, gesturing for calm and less noise, for holding back and for better control. There he was, once or twice turning his back to see if he could catch another quick look at his past. Of course the visitors had the right of way out. He could not help himself. He gave a quick furtive look down my row of standing girls. We locked eyes. I wished I could stick my tongue out at him. There was still the Sunday morning service before the departure of the visitors but it was now just a few days before we went home for the long holidays. I ached to speak to my mother and tell her I had seen the man who used to live in our yard in Alexandra.

❖❖❖

ON 5 DECEMBER 1956, South Africa woke up to the news that a wave of arrests had taken place almost simultaneously all over the country. As many as 156 leaders of the main political organisations – Africans, Indians, coloureds and whites, male and female – had all been picked up in the early hours of the morning and jailed. Among the detained was Chief Albert Luthuli, the leader of the ANC, a friend of the American Board of Missions and an annual guest speaker at Inanda. It was just before the Christmas break, when we would all be going home for the long summer holidays. When Dr Scott made the announcement at morning assembly a day later, the excitement of the impending vacation was replaced by anxiety and great fear. Our familiarity with treason was limited to our English and Zulu literary studies, and we knew that the charge was a good pretext for beheading the accused.

The following year, when we had settled back into school, we were told that a special visitor, who would remain nameless, would be spending the weekend at the school. The weekend guests of Dr Scott or the staff usually arrived on Friday evening while we were in the dining room. I did not see him arrive but soon the school was abuzz with rumours from those who had caught a glimpse of him. I will never forget that short scene at the Sunday service. Dr Scott, going to the podium more sombrely than usual, speaking in a staccato voice, said something like this: 'Today we have a special visitor. He has been banned by the South African government. He cannot be in a room with more than two people. He is not allowed to address a meeting. This will be the first time he has been among us and cannot address us. But we could not let him leave without greeting you.' We all turned our heads towards the aisle, expecting the visitor to enter through the main door and walk towards the nave. But there was nothing. There was a door on either side of the altar. Both doors opened almost simultaneously and a shaft of sunlight bathed the altar. A grey-haired, very handsome man entered through the side door. He was wearing a white shirt and a dark suit. He did not appear to be in a hurry. It was as if we had caught sight of him in the middle of a normal outing. So he continued apace, across the altar, waving his hand, and his face turned towards the congregation, in a smile. It was Chief Albert Luthuli. Slowly, he strode across the stage, nodding towards the thundering applause, screams and foot-stamping from the full house of Inanda girls. He did not say a word. He just waved his hand as he walked away, through to the open door, and out into the open air.

In my head it has remained one of the greatest speeches never made. That cameo of a silent, middle-aged man walking across a stage in a room filled with cheering, tearful, militant young women is unforgettable. That was the hidden magic of Inanda. It imposed constraints, but we were free to take the reminder that we were part of the big world outside, where our work had been cut out for us.

So, in the five years I spent there, some of the most interesting people in South Africa were invited to come and address us about their work experience in politics, social work, missionary work and the like. The strictly segregated, ethnically based Bantu universities had become a reality. Significantly, they were also to become the bedrock of the Black Consciousness Movement, which radically redefined the self-identity of Africans and resuscitated the resistance movement that had been bashed into the underground, left for dead. The spirit of Steve Biko lives in the pantheon of our national heritage with all the greats of our country – Mandela, Sisulu, Ngoyi, and a thousand, thousand others before and after them, those who sang, who made images, who danced, who ran, who fell and got up, who wrote, who fought, who brought us to the here and now.

The overwhelming emotion about my five years at Inanda is ambivalence. In the end I both loved it and hated it. The school archives have preserved every record of my life there. My end-of-term reports, my participation in school activities, the letters between my mother and Dr Scott. Even after my departure I kept in touch with Dr Scott, advising her of my parents' divorce and my plans to study abroad. It is clear in her thoughtfully composed responses that she sought to anchor me. In a sense the school represents the most stable and reliable influence in my life. I attribute my moral standards to the valuable example of my family, the Masekelas, who actively contributed to the well-being of the communities they lived in. But those lessons were reinforced and entrenched at Inanda. Even my political beliefs, which were seeded in Alexandra, found sustenance at Inanda, where every effort was made to emphasise the equality of races. As for gender equality, where else could I have had a better example of the capability of women but at Inanda, which was administered by women missionaries, all of them celibate but most of them holding high academic achievements and almost ruthless in their ambition for us to walk in the light of knowledge and morality?

FIVE

THE GAP YEAR

AMONG THE small number of Africans who completed university studies, almost all depended on funding from charitable organisations. The story within the story of graduation day celebrations is the cameo of the widowed or single mother who put her son or daughter through higher education by doing the laundry or cleaning the houses of white folks.

Our society, based on white supremacy and the systemic economic deprivation of blacks, produced only a handful of affluent Africans who could afford to put their children through tertiary education. We had neither a merchant class nor a landed gentry. A few Africans with independent means were self-made farmers who had managed to hold on to land with the assistance of missionaries or through the privilege of traditional colonial arrangements. Of course, there were exceptions, such as businessmen, herbalists, shamans, heads of independent religious formations, confidence tricksters and the like. Their deeds were on everybody's tongues, as the saying went. They featured in magazine articles as 'tycoons' or 'moguls', medicine men posing near their 'mansions' or brand-new cars that were described as 'out of the box'.

All the cars my father owned were second-hand. The black Wolseley was totally unfit for the potholed streets of Alexandra, and it became a ritual for the whole family, including Mama in her Sunday best, to push-start it with my father at the steering wheel. It was not unusual for the car to break down in the middle of a township like Evaton, Atteridgeville or Benoni. When he was seized by the angels or the demons of the past, we were captives in the vehicle, as he manoeuvred over the potholes of the untarred township streets in search of some person or some sight to rekindle the memory of a time before we existed. Unabashed, he did not hesitate to recruit whoever was on the street to help him push-start the car. All dressed up, my mother, my sisters and I would disembark from the car and wait on a strange street. There for all to see was Papa, his good jacket abandoned in the back seat, half of his body inside the car, steering, and the other half outside the car, pushing, together with the Good Samaritans, as the car retched and groaned, jerking its way around the block. Both young and old boys seemed to enjoy the distraction of helping out and the sound of the gurgling engine coming alive again brought smiles of accomplishment to their faces. The job done, no one lingered, waiting to be paid, no one held out an open hand to be rewarded for being of assistance. But my father always handed out some silver coins to the young ones, even though it was generally understood that there was no entitlement to payment for aiding someone in need and it did not matter whether the car was a *skoro-skoro* or recently out of the box. We waited unafraid in the street, secure in the unseen presence of onlookers peeping through the nylon lace curtains, or a granny there, her legs outstretched on the unfolded grass mat, with young ones hovering around her under the single family tree in the yard.

Under the bright sunlight of a late Sunday afternoon, in that dense arrangement of houses all alike in rows, there was always some activity taking place. Across the narrow street a rusty gate creaked as a little boy pushed it open, a group of prayer women in colourful blouses matched with black skirts thumped their hymn books in joyous song, separating like the tributaries of a river to find their ways home as the sound of their till-next-times gradually dimmed to nothing, and a lone dog barked for attention. We stood there, hiding our impatience, ready to jump into the car while the engine was still running. Inside the car once more we pretended not to hear a new-sounding rattle emanating from another part of the engine. We raised our brows and moved our eyes in a dance of anxiety about the possibility of yet another breakdown.

At first these breakdowns were a joke, then they became an irritation, which grew into a refusal from my mother, who would no longer accompany Papa on his nostalgic visits to homes they had lived in as young marrieds or to see the original sights he was continually discovering. I became the one who would be volunteered to go with my father, and he taught me how to wonder. He tutored me to marry my senses to the colours, the light and shapes around me and to understand that every space could provide an escape from the mundane, if you looked. Intent on discovery, he always found something new in his God's world and, as in his early sculpting, he hardly paused to finish one thing before he went on to start a new one. He revelled in the abundance of novelty, and as a religious man he saw it as an ultimate gift from his God. He did not need or desire any more.

Among his children I learnt how to dirty my hands in the soil and make a garden where I could play with colour. I remember that he would rise alone before dawn to collect smooth, black pebbles and they shone brightly on the side of the pond where the goldfish ducked and dived in the shadows of the water lilies. One of the presents he bought me that I have never forgotten is a kaleidoscope that he brought to KwaGuqa for my tenth birthday.

I attribute my love of ethnic cultural design to his early obsession with African masks, set against the clays, grasses and unpolished metals of the continent. I still delight in the sudden burst of brilliant colour woven into any old garment from the east, west, south or north, and favour the sunburnt soil that is reflected in the setting sun just before it dips into the dark. Papa scouted certain neighbourhoods for beautiful architectural designs and he was notorious for his unexpected visits to artists he admired. He disarmed the 'owners' by his curiosity, his interest in their work. Despite themselves, they were flattered by his genuine admiration of the artistic objects they had made.

No one in my family owned land or had a university degree. Yet we were considered better off because both of my parents had professional jobs and my aunts and uncles were all employed, with my uncle in Springs considered a wealthy man because he ran a successful grocery store. By 1960, in a population of over seventeen million people, dominated by a five per cent white minority owning eighty-seven per cent of the land, a fixture of African society was a robust popular urban press. In *The Bantu World*, *Zonk!*, *Drum*, *Golden City Press* and *Ilanga Lase Natal*, we read about self-styled township Robin Hoods, executed tsotsis, entertainment figures like Todd Matshikiza, the Manhattan Brothers, Miriam Makeba, Paul Robeson and many others, sports figures like Joe Louis, and political leaders like Sisulu, Mandela, Trevor Huddleston, Lillian Ngoyi, Kwame Nkrumah and Seretse Khama. All were presented to us in racy language and vivid photographs.

In 1960, when I matriculated from Inanda Seminary, the acquisition of a BA or a BSc degree was still the highest realistic academic aspiration for an African and considered a passport to success. But this had been tarnished by the aggressive imposition of the Bantu Education Act, now augmented by the Extension of

University Education Act of 1959, explicitly intended to separate Africans in higher education from the universally held norms of academic freedom. Four of my five years at Inanda had been dominated by the Treason Trial, and during that time the political opposition in the form of peaceful civil disobedience against passes, low wages and the like had spread in dramatic proportions. The unexpected development was of women in rural areas mounting an unprecedented campaign against carrying passes. It was inspired by the ongoing protests of the ANC Women's League and the Federation of South African Women, and yet it had its own momentum, fuelled by the women's determination not to suffer the same fate as their menfolk under the pass laws.

The so-called influx control of blacks seeking employment in the urban areas was the cause of great calamity to rural women. They and their children were viewed as surplus, inessential to the economic needs of white South Africa, and through the extension of the pass laws to women it became the intention of the law to dump them in the rural areas, which lacked all the basic necessities for a decent, dignified and safe life.

There were hardly any social facilities in the reserves, and the arid, tired soil could yield no sustenance for the inhabitants. My parents, like other African civil servants all over the country, were the de facto instruments for implementing apartheid policies. Irrespective of their personal oppositional views they were the messengers who interpreted apartheid to its victims, explaining to widowed women why they could not remain in the towns or own the houses they lived in because they were minors, telling the old men they must leave the towns because they were no longer of any use in the factories, the mines or the gardens. It was heart-rending work, even for the pastor, the teacher, the nurse, the breaking of the spirit of those who had been trained in church and in school to serve the interests of the disadvantaged.

They were now turned into the parrots of doom, repeating empty phrases about the law says this and the law says that and there is nothing we can do.

Undeterred by repressive legislation, the resistance movement had drawn greater numbers of supporters beyond the urban areas into the very hinterland of the country, where spectacular protests were staged. At Inanda Seminary, there was unvarnished support for Chief Albert Luthuli. One of our strictest teachers, Edith Sibisi, married MB Yengwa, who was then provincial secretary of the Natal ANC, a Defiance Campaign organiser and detainee as well as a Treason Trialist. The unfolding political events like the Sharpeville Massacre, followed by the banning of the ANC and the PAC in April 1960, the declaration of a state of emergency and other related events, were announced at assembly on a regular basis, and we held intense discussions among ourselves about the situation. Every one of us knew of someone who had been questioned or arrested by the police, and we knew that none of us would, in our life outside the boundaries of Inanda, be exempt from the long tentacles of apartheid security.

As with all missionary schools, Inanda was under threat of closure unless the school agreed to fall under the control of the Bantu Education tsar. Dr Scott wrestled with the dilemma of how to continue the school, founded in 1853, without compromising the values that were espoused by its own board members, like Chief Albert Luthuli. We were teenagers on the verge of adulthood, and the glaring reality of repression was the only future awaiting us outside the boundaries of Inanda. Thousands had been detained across the country, many subjected to horrendous physical brutality, including torture. This could be our fate too in the world outside Inanda.

Some of the leaders of the liberation movement left the country to pursue the fight against the regime when it became clear that the peaceful means of waging opposition were being rendered futile by the increasing severity of the regime, which was now using execution as a deterrent to political activism as well as solitary confinement and torture for up to 180 days in its arsenal of repression. The involvement in the liberation struggle of Manto Mali and Joyce Sikhakhane was an inspiration to me and it was a concrete example of the Inanda motto, 'Shine where you are'. In particular, Manto was the epitome of the softly spoken, law-abiding and compassionate senior student. None of us ever suspected that she was an ANC member, and her departure from the country to join the movement in exile, being one of the few women to do so, made us proud.

A people familiar with the harshness and cruelty of successive chapters of white rule, through centuries, we could never have imagined the unspeakable atrocities that were yet to be devised and used against us. Revelations of hideous new forms of torture on both men and women, the use of experts from right-wing regimes in Latin America to inculcate the arts of abomination into local security forces, and the refinement and expansion of the arms industry with technical development assistance from 'civilised' countries were a clear indication of how far our white rulers would go to find a final solution to the *swart gevaar* – which they had now dressed in bloody red to suit the theatre of the Cold War. It was not well in our communities, and everywhere in South Africa there was a deep sense of disquiet. But there was also a growing common purpose among the oppressed, there was courage, and there was the inspiration of the African independence movement that was sprouting all over the continent. It was a promise of things to come.

Despite the elaborate propaganda of 'separate but equal', the fact was that the minority regime was brutally repressive and exploitative, and in blatant violation of the human rights of the majority and those who supported them. They were fuelling a race war that could only result in a bloodbath. This would not benefit anyone, including the profiteers masquerading as investors. Those resisting apartheid had a moral upper hand and, with Oliver Tambo at the helm of the ANC in exile, people across the world, in all their social, political and economic formations, began to take on the fight as their own, demanding economic, diplomatic and political sanctions against apartheid. When the United Nations declared apartheid a crime against humanity, light was shone on the darkest corners of suffering in South African prisons, townships, reserves and workplaces. The nefarious deeds of the apartheid regime were no longer a secret. No one could claim they did not know. The ownership of suffering spread fast as more and more people learnt of apartheid's heinous rule. The condemnations increased in proportion to the regime's vociferous claims that theirs was a last stand against communism.

Governments that were apologists for the regime, or outright supporters, began to waver because of the pressure exerted by their own citizens, who repudiated any form of cooperation with apartheid. Under stringent political conditions, many professionals, including academics, writers and journalists, were leaving the country because the laws of the country prevented them from expressing the truth they saw. They had no freedom of association and the right to protest against injustice had been 'legislated' away. The police had the right to arrest, charge and punish 'offenders'. Under the militarised administration, the notorious secret service held sway over all matters deemed 'terrorist'. No longer permitted to speak the names of certain individuals, to read certain books, or even to sing certain songs, spied on and hounded at every turn, insulted and debased by the rule of warped law, citizens opted out to help spread the word about their home. They left to grow their voices again and shout out, together with others who shared the same values and whom they would find wherever they went. They fled from toxic seeds germinated in the dry earth sprinkled by tears, from this place where their afterbirth was buried. The call to arms was declared and what had been a peaceful, persuasive struggle was built on a new pillar of armed struggle. Those who left hoped to return, confident that in five or six years, or even fewer, their own fighting for freedom in support of the overwhelming majority of people at home and the solidarity of those abroad would break the strength of the regime. But it would be more than three decades before the first democratic elections in South Africa.

The right to a national passport came to the fore as a growing number of known political activists were refused passports to travel outside the country. Some left the country secretly while others chose to apply for exit permits and lost their citizenship.

At Inanda the younger students were bolder in their condemnation of the Bantu universities, calling them puppet schools in puppet states, terms popularly used at political meetings and repeated in the press. At home during my last winter holiday from boarding school, I refused to make an application to enter Turfloop University. The prospect of being restricted to my ethnic group in an ethnic university located in what the regime had determined to be my special homeland was anathema to me. Having been exposed to girls from all over South Africa at Inanda, having studied the Zulu language and literature for five years, I had become more a product of the school than of my father's tribe. I would come to identify more with Nomthandazo Shezi, Edith Sibisi Yengwa and Joyce Sikhakhane. Joyce had entered the school as I was about to leave it. She came from an activist ANC family in Soweto and was very voluble in her repudiation of the special education that would be imposed in the tribal Bantustans. She was a precursor to the firebrands of the school uprisings in Soweto, Bonteheuwel and all over

South Africa, and in 1976 a fearless generation of students confronted the onslaught of the police and their trained dogs, and then the army, with only their bodies and stones.

❖ ❖ ❖

IT WAS very easy to adapt to the prayerful serenity of Inanda, and nearly all of the senior students belonged to the SCA and never broke rules or attracted attention to themselves. I went through a phase in my third year when I considered becoming a missionary. Seeing the missionaries every day, going through the routine of work and prayer, wearing the same colourless clothes and preaching the same gospel, provoked our curiosity. There was little or no occasion for us to get to know them as women – they were frozen in the holier-than-thou role of spirituality and service, estranged from passion and free from longing. Only Miss Cheyney played her heart out during the services at the chapel. Under her pumping feet, the organ would groan, whimper, screech and bellow out emotion so bare that a look of worry would cross Dr Scott's brow. One of the older girls would remark, '*Ukhumbule kude namhlanje uMam*.' (Her mind is in a faraway place today.)

We wondered whether the missionaries were one another's keepers, if they curbed each other. None of them ever spoke of home or shared their news with us, yet they knew everything about us. We wondered about their personal lives and projected our own theories about what had pushed them into a life of sacrifice and service. I was attracted to the insularity of their private lives and resented the continuous intrusions into my own. At the time of wishing to escape the pain and ugliness of my disintegrating home, it was seductive to imagine a life of aloneness where my only commitment would be to assist the downtrodden and where I could be impervious to personal emotional pain.

A walk that I had taken to the village, beyond the boundaries of the school, was a step towards reclaiming my free will to choose my own path to adulthood and the responsibility for my own actions.

I had always thought that my departure from Inanda would be the happiest day of my life, yet when the time came to leave I felt drawn especially towards my teachers, knowing that they loved the school in me – and that, like the child I was to my parents, I would always remain an Inanda girl to the seminary.

BACK HOME in Natalspruit the mood was pretty glum and I was not keen to play my previous role of peacemaker between my parents. At any hour of the night or in the early hours of the morning, alone in my room with the kitchen between me and my parents in their room, I could hear them arguing, their voices rising dangerously. Mercifully, there was no physical violence. My mother was still active in the National Council of African Women and could devote a lot of her spare time to the organisation because my younger sisters were with Ouma. My father missed his younger daughters and felt outwitted and robbed of his authority as a father and a husband. On those weekends when we visited Ouma and my sisters, he would insist on driving us there. It did not help that he was a poor driver and that we winced and held our breath every time he swerved to avoid an obstacle and almost landed us in a ditch on the side of the road. That was about the only time the three of us still did anything together, when we rode in the car to Ouma's house in Grasmere.

It was a far cry from the time when I had first gone to live with my parents in Alexandra. We did not sing in the car and we did not converse with each other. Each parent would direct a comment to me, and no matter how much my response enveloped them both, my parents remained apart, each wrapped and locked in a separate silence. Here in the semi-rural environment, thirty miles south of Johannesburg, in an all-female household on Ouma's acre of land and under her roof, I was better able to feel a sense of belonging. I felt an easy camaraderie with Ouma, although she did not approve of my smoking cigarettes and my 'running around in the streets' going to the bioscope and concerts with boys whose families were unknown. What disgusted her most was when I described eating at Kapitan's restaurant on Kort Street in Johannesburg. She swore that she could never eat food with unknown customers, prepared by strangers in dubious premises with hygiene uncertainties. But she was no longer the forceful matriarch who ruled everyone, and all of us under her roof, my mother and my sisters, cajoled her with exaggerated accounts of the new city life led by blacks. Her reaction was indulgent, a performance of disdain not unmixed with the desire to amuse as she called out loud for her ancestors in isiNdebele. Leaving KwaGuqa had been a rupture with her whole past. She had been separated from her remaining relatives, in particular my beloved Ouma Sussie. When the municipality began to tear down the old location and move people to Lynnville, Ouma Sussie also moved. She went to live with her daughter Auntie Lily in Roodepoort, whose husband Uncle Nico worked at Durban Deep.

Eager to embrace my brother's life in music, I had befriended musicians like Bea Benjamin and Dollar Brand, and had even brought them home to Grassies, as we fondly called Ouma's new home. My other friends, like Yolisa Bokwe, Nat Nakasa and Joe Louw, had also had occasion to be hosted at Ouma's house. Most of my father's family and Ouma's made their way to Grasmere to see Ouma, and there was never an effort to deny our true identity. At nineteen I was able to weave in and out of the various social groups mainly because I could speak English, Afrikaans and Sesotho with fluency. In addition, the isiNdebele I had learnt as a child in KwaGuqa was the foundation upon which my five years study of Zulu language and literature at Inanda had been laid. Not so for my two younger sisters who, like many of their generation, became the victims of a system that distorted reality and made them witness to the shattering and scattering of not only our family, but a whole nation. Somehow, in my peripatetic growing up, from Witbank to Alexandra to Inanda and back to Johannesburg, I had adapted to the authority of shifting: as I looked at the stories of my whole family, of whole groups of people in my country, it was clear that moving from one place to the other, whether voluntarily or under coercion, led to change. So, however much Johanna mocked my father for being a rolling stone, I still considered it better than being stuck in KwaGuqa as a child, or in Alexandra, or Inanda, or Johannesburg, or New York, or Lusaka.

When Ouma first moved to Grasmere, almost everybody there lived in the perfect isolation of colouredness, enjoying the perks of more pay, access to white liquor, access to electricity and water, unaffected by the raging war against apartheid. Prior to the 1948 elections, in every coloured township there were people who still held strong links with their rural African background. They spoke African languages without shame and did not regard themselves as above the blacks. Tragically, apartheid policies pursued a naked divide-and-rule strategy that, for many decades, splintered the society into self-interested segments — with the whites superimposed over everyone. The new protocol for coloureds was to be ignorant and take pride in their ignorance of everything African.

Now, for the first time in her life, Ouma was not earning her own living. She had succeeded in qualifying for a coloured pension, which was much more generous than that given to Africans. The idea of starting a tavern in Grasmere had been shot down by my mother. It would jeopardise her case to gain custody of the two younger children in the upcoming divorce. Besides, there was enough land to grow food. With my father's botanical expertise and Ouma's inclination towards hard work and self-reliance, the acre of land was transformed into a family food basket. They grew an orchard with apricot, peach, pomegranate and fig trees, medicinal and cooking herbs, and vegetables, including a small corn field.

The only remaining evidence of that era is an overgrown rosemary bush, a stubborn artemisia, a sad pomegranate and a denuded fig tree that bears no fruit. Ouma's property, now unfenced and bounded by 7th and 8th Avenues, has become a thoroughfare, a short cut through which neighbours of all ages, alone and in groups, stroll on their way to the shop on the opposite side of the street and on their way home. It is a bleak reminder of a vengeful legacy that would fix all people of colour in a position of poverty and financial insecurity. With no generational wealth to insure whatever rudimentary wealth they may have held, they would always revert to poverty. The death or the illness of the main wage earner would invariably threaten the status of the dependants and lead to indigence. So, when my mother died in 1983, it was the beginning of the end of Ouma's security. To make ends meet, portions of the land were sold until now all that remains is half an acre, left in her will to her twelve great-grandchildren.

❖❖❖

IN 1961, Johannesburg was still the fashion centre of South Africa. The garment sector, then the fourth-largest industry in South

Africa, employed thousands of women of all races in its factories. It was Auntie May, a friend of Mama's in Grasmere, who got me a job in a factory in the city. She belonged to a trade union and was a shop steward. The rage that summer was spaghetti-strap dresses. My job was to empty the tray of mounds of the narrow-sewn lengths straight from the machinist, turn them inside out and place them on a tray to my right, where they were picked up and then attached to the finished bodices of the dresses. Everyone was so intent on their particular part of the relay, and so pushed to keep the race of production unbroken, that there was no time to chat. What mattered most was to stay on time and keep your job. At the end of the morning I would rush out of the room with everybody to take a break and to grab something to eat. I was nineteen years old but in the same rush outdoors were older women with daughters and grandchildren, as well as their own mothers and fathers, all waiting to be fed.

The work was hard for everyone and there was no special attention for new workers. That is where I started smoking cigarettes, in solidarity with my workmates. Perhaps it distracted me from the physical pain in my fingers and my legs, or helped to ease the distress caused by my parents' impending separation, but it certainly brought me acceptance in my new environment. Among the workers in this factory the majority of the women were coloured but there was not a hint of racism. Here, nobody cared about straight hair, the colour of your skin or your eyes, or whether you were a matriculant. Every day I stood at the small table, not even high enough to rest my elbows on, going through the same mechanical motions, turning out hundreds of straps in perfect time to keep up with the machinists, who had a quota to complete every day.

In every factory in every town, workers went through repetitive tasks every day for eight or more hours. Some of the young

African women who worked in the garment industry were icons of style in the townships. They specialised in wearing tailored clothes made of pure wool, silk or cotton. Gabardine, tweed, mohair and cashmere, these were the coveted fabrics in winter, just as cotton, silk, corduroy and flannel were commonly admired. Clothing lasted a lifetime, and an inherited suit or any other item made from natural fibre was considered a major acquisition. Alterations were the norm and the use of dry cleaners was a budgetary prerequisite for any self-respecting city dresser. The shift to synthetic fabrics like nylon and terylene, which were 'wash and dry', soon became all the rage, but was met with great disdain by the older generation, who valued durability and quality. Ouma stuck to her cotton-knit navy bloomers and flannel petticoats for underwear until we moved to Alexandra, when Mama bought her two sets of nylon underwear – which she hated – for special occasions.

It was only in her prayers that my granny was vulnerable and when she questioned why her lot in life had been so joyless and so dominated by hard, unrewarding work. Almost every night she inveighed bitterly against her Maker, asking why Khalo had been snatched away from her, why Walter had left her to raise the children alone. Her interior life was inhabited almost solely by Walter, Khalo and my mother. This was what had brought me closer to her, when I began to understand that she was impervious to sticks and stones but a small thing could render her grossly out of control – like when she had suddenly burst out crying because a crepe-de-Chine dress delivered for her to wear to Auntie Dolly's wedding did not fit her. The mourning period after the death of her brother Oupa Jacobus and Khalo had just been observed. Khalo had been killed less than two months after her brother had died. The black clothes had been washed ceremoniously and packed away. Now, this first deep-coloured dress would not go over her hips smoothly and the pleat down the front had no room to lie flat. Everything was skew and the hem barely covered her knees.

She just sat on the chair in front of the mirror after she had pulled the dress off, over her head.

'I am not going to this wedding. Go with the others, Babsie.'

Then she wept soundlessly, her shoulders shaking violently just like that day – 20 December 1948 – when we had got the telegram about Khalo, the tears just dropping down her face.

As I grew older I became witness to other occasions when her dammed emotions burst the containing walls of endurance, but this occasion was like an ambush, marring the role I was to play that day as flower girl at the wedding. Her flare-up singed me, and I understood how much she hurt and how much she hated everyone in the room knowing it. When they killed her son in Brakpan, they broke her strength. She had not rehearsed for the occasion because, as the mourners had said, it was not a natural occurrence – parents were not meant to bury their children.

Even now, nearly seventy years later, some rare scene of Ouma, her fragility laid bare, pushes to the front of my mind. I see her without her bluff of toughness. It is almost as if my memory compels me to see our life together in a better light, and I wonder if she guessed that my judgement and resentment of her – and the fact that I lacked the compassion that she had withheld from me, and that I replaced it with unforgiving hardness – were because I had no one to turn to who could have understood. Children had no rights or opinions, just as their parents had few choices.

'*Dit sal regkom*, Jwi. (It will be all right.) Babsie, *laat ons gaan*. (Let us go.)'

That was my Ouma Sussie, always smoothing out difficulties, shying away from confrontation.

❖❖❖

I HAD a chance to think a lot at my factory job. It helped to
pass the long, brutal hours when time seemed to stand still. I was
able to stick it out because I knew it was not to be a lifetime
occupation, I would not have to endure it forever, this gap year,
and the long letters from my brother were enthusiastic about my
being able to study abroad. For almost three months I endured
this numbing work until Auntie May heard of another job. This
time, it was an opening in the subscriptions department of the
New Age newspaper. It was a frequently banned publication that
had changed its name but retained its militancy: at its inception
in the early 1950s it was called *The Guardian*, then renamed
Advance, only to be resurrected again as the *New Age*.

By now, with the help of Nat Nakasa, I had found a room in
Berea, in the house of a Jewish woman who was living with an
African actor. His reputation was growing and he was to become
a leading man in several popular South African films. Mama
agreed with me that my father was not to know about my tenancy
in Berea. The rent was nominal because I had a special 'stand-in'
role to play in case of a police raid. My part was that, in the event
of a police raid, to avoid charges under the Immorality Act, I was
to act as the maid employed by the woman and the actor as my
live-in boyfriend. I was thrilled to have my own place to stay and
it was fortunate that there was never a raid as we had never got
around to rehearsing an arrest scene. But alone at night, after a
long day at the factory, I would go over and over the role I had
played in the separation of my parents.

It had all happened unexpectedly. I was propelled by something I had not yet given a name, which resided deeply in me
and whose insistence I could not ignore. It made me fearless. It
was early in the morning on a workday. The three of us were still

together in Natalspruit. They were shouting at each other again. It was as if they were addressing me directly. I sprang out of bed and, without knocking, flung their bedroom door wide open. I expected the worst but there was no blood.

'Stop it, stop it at once! If you can't live together, why can't you part in peace?'

I was so shocked by what I had said that I started to tremble in fear, expecting my father to turn on me for my disrespect. I backed out of their room and fled to mine, where I immediately started packing a bag. I heard my father bang the kitchen door and the car starting. He drove away.

She was sitting on the bed.

'I am going away, to Ouma or to Uncle Kenny. I can't live like this any more.'

We left together, to Ouma. There had been no time to ponder the meaning of my decision and the weight of racial baggage in my family. That my mother's consideration of divorce also entailed a choice to be reclassified as a coloured, and that custody of my sisters would mean that my father would be an outsider. In retrospect, I see that the acquisition of my own place to live was also meant to distance myself from any perception that I was in wholesale agreement with my mother's position in the marital war. I had long since healed from the cuts and bruises of my year at the City and Suburban Coloured School, but the fact is that I had experienced firsthand the bigotry begotten by the distorted racial wars of apartheid, which pitted wife against husband, child against parent and neighbour against neighbour. Living in town I could go to restaurants, movies and jazz shows without worrying about the curfew and getting back to the township. I was hanging out with journalists and musicians after work, and at *New Age* my boss in the subscriptions department was Wolfie Kodesh. But the real action was in the office on the opposite side of the reception desk, where Ruth First and Ahmed Kathrada always seemed to be in serious discussion about the next edition of the newspaper, with no interest in our work. Rica Hodgson, Mary and Ben Turok, the Weinbergs, Walter Sisulu, Govan Mbeki and all the big names in the Congress of Democrats were regulars at the office. I remember distinctly that Rica Hodgson and Ruth First were always very chic, but while Rica was cheery and outgoing, Ruth was very serious. One of the journalists was a slight, keen-eyed young poet named William Kgositsile, and together with Joyce Mohamed, Esther Mtshali and Thandi Rankoe we would all go to MACOSA House for social evenings organised by the ANC Youth League, whose members included Sindiso Mfenyana, Thabo Mbeki and Aziz Pahad.

One afternoon, my father arrived at my workplace unannounced. I was nonchalantly smoking a cigarette, which I thought of throwing down – but on second thoughts I just held on to the cigarette and continued smoking, expecting the worst from him. He said nothing and on his next visit he brought me a packet of twenty Peter Stuyvesant filter cigarettes. At the time, my father did not know that I was living in my own place.

My progress at work was good and soon I was doing fieldwork, going on door-to-door visits in the townships to get people to subscribe to the newspaper's annual Christmas hamper. It entitled each subscriber to a free copy of the *New Age* paper if they purchased a Christmas hamper on a monthly instalment plan. It was a brave enterprise that focused on informing the public that the struggle was alive and well, despite the arrests, bannings and deepening repression. Even more significantly, it shed light on other struggles on the continent, helping to engender the spirit of international solidarity. *New Age* readers could learn about people's activities in the far-flung townships of all the provinces. One issue even showed a march of multitudes to the

Bastille in France, in support of the Movement for Democracy and against the far-right anti-independence OAS in Algeria. These stories about independence in the former colonies of Europe were a source of great encouragement to the people, as were the stories about South African political leaders who were now outside the country and the boycott campaigns they were pursuing in their host countries. Most prominently, it was an anti-apartheid newspaper that had survived many bannings by changing its name each time it was banned. It highlighted the anti-government activities of the opposition, which was still alive despite the banning of the ANC and the SACP.

I had other clandestine errands that Wolfie Kodesh sent me on, errands like making phone calls from public telephone booths and leaving cryptic messages. I suspected that the other girls were also carrying out duties unconnected to newspaper subscriptions, but we did not share information. When I met him again in Cape Town, more than twenty-seven years later, neither of us could remember the details of the messages – and that is how it was meant to be, anyway. There were only two or three of these assignments, but I would leave the phone booth with a racing heart, making my way back to the office on a roundabout route, trying hard to act indifferent. It never occurred to me that I could be arrested and interrogating the messages was the last thing on my mind. I just knew they were important and felt proud that I could deliver them.

My emancipation from parental control had been swift and unplanned. The outburst at my parents was like a formal transition from an emotional attachment. Some hierarchical barrier had been broken and I recognised my own power to influence events without pandering to some unwritten law requiring fake respect.

Almost twenty years old, I now had the opportunity to define my life according to my own precepts. I had been groomed by Uncle Kenny to regard myself as different from other women of my age. He stressed that I was more articulate and intelligent, and would never be able to settle into the humdrum ways of ordinary township life. Even when I was a child in KwaGuqa, my uncle would time his unexpected visits to coincide with my school holidays and, sweeping Ouma's excuses aside, have my bags packed and drive off with me to his home in Springs. When I was driven back, his DKW would be full of packages of clothes and toys for me. Once, he even bought me a bicycle.

I never cried when my uncle left me back in KwaGuqa. I was always filled with awe and confidence, because he always came back for me. We would pay a surprise visit to my parents in Alexandra, who would be astounded by my appearance. According to our Setlokwa custom, my father's brothers were my fathers and their children were my brothers and my sisters. Uncle Kenny delighted in the exclamations of my parents as we made our surprise entrance. Those were the best times of my childhood, and I never felt sad about waving goodbye to my parents as the case would be when they would leave KwaGuqa after a visit.

Uncle Kenny healed the deep feelings of orphanhood that used to wrack my body into an upheaval of shivers and hiccups long after the tears had gone. I loved him almost as much as I loved my brother, and my life afterwards, as a growing adult, would always be lacking without either of them. No one ever measured up to their high standing in my universe. So, as I entered the stage of courtship, my yardstick shifted and slid to approximate the wit, the humour and the swaggering intelligence of those two: there was always something wanting in my suitors.

Many journalists came to the *New Age* offices to verify and follow up on stories, not least to get information about arrested leaders and other activists – the editor Fred Carneson, for instance. Like many others who visited the office, Carneson had been a Treason Trialist, arrested over sixty times for his political activities. He was on trial for refusing to reveal the sources of a story in the paper. Young journalists at *Drum* magazine, *Golden City Post* and the like often came to our offices to meet with Joe Gqabi or Ruth First. Govan Mbeki, who was on the *New Age* editorial board and was based in the Eastern Cape, was a frequent visitor.

As a new employee, I was not familiar with many of the activists who closed the door behind them when they entered Ruth and Kathy Kathrada's office. They were well known to Joyce Mohamed and to Esther Mtshali, my colleagues who were in the inner circles of the movement. I met Nat Nakasa at the *New Age* offices. Like many journalists, he had come to get information about a story.

The most frequent visitors were lawyers and trade union members. I recognised people like Walter Sisulu, Nelson Mandela, Titus Nkobi and Duma Nokwe from my childhood days when they addressed ANC meetings at the square in Alexandra near 12th Avenue, and from photographs in the newspapers. The atmosphere at the office was very relaxed. I do not remember being vetted or questioned about my background, and I never witnessed a quarrel among the comrades or sensed the existence of a cult surrounding any of the leaders. Nor was there any open demonstration of hierarchy. Despite the deepening repression and the growing number of arrests, there was a cheerful air that ruled the interactions that were focused on the liberation struggle.

Soon I was riding on the back of Nat's scooter and accompanying him to shebeens in Johannesburg and Soweto. Ours was more of a companionship than a love affair. I remember that he came to pick me up for a date once, all agog because he had met the daughter of one of the wealthiest men in South Africa and she had agreed to go on a date with him. It did not affect me; in the short time I had known him, I had learnt that he was a sucker for short-lived infatuations that soon petered out. He took me to my first 'mixed party' at the home of Nadine Gordimer. Nat was greatly influenced by his homeboy Lewis Nkosi, for whom he had great regard and admiration. Nkosi had introduced him to the Johannesburg scene and it was not long before he developed his own professional and social reputation. For one, he managed to win my father over and became a family friend rather than a suitor. Both my parents spoke freely to him about their work in the Natalspruit Municipality. He had liaisons with other women and never made a secret of it, but he liked my company and we became very close friends and intellectual mates who shared opinions about books and writers.

It is during this time that I first met Yolisa Bokwe, with whom I have shared a friendship for over sixty years. Originally from Middeldrift in the Eastern Cape, she came to Johannesburg from Birmingham in England where she had studied classical music. She taught the piano at Dorkay House. Nat Nakasa took one look at this sophisticated, petite beauty and fell in love. I met her in Robinson Deep through Joyce Piliso, who was a neighbour of friends of my parents, the Denalanes. We still roll about laughing remembering the story of my arrest. It was a Sunday morning and I was at Yolisa's cottage in a backyard in Parktown. There was a knock at the door and when Yoli opened it a big white policeman shadowed the way and demanded to know what we were doing in a white area. He took our passes and we were under arrest. As we waited for the police van to arrive, Yoli asked the policeman if she could go to the lavatory. He agreed, rather too readily. It was the custom of the police, then, to drive around all day collecting suspects and only to return to the police station when the van was full. This was to be our fate too, but there was no Yolisa to be my partner in 'crime' that day: she had climbed through the toilet window and escaped.

It was only when the van arrived with two more constables that it dawned on me that she had gone. I felt abandoned and betrayed as I bounced up and down in the empty van, which stopped periodically to pick up more reluctant passengers. Eventually, at dusk, after my charges were confirmed, I was taken to the women's prison, where the Constitutional Court is now located. I prepared myself for my first night in prison – ablution bucket, clanging doors and all. The cell reeked of dirt, dust, sweat and urine, and for the first time it dawned on me that I really was under arrest.

As I was coming to terms with my plight there was a noise at the door, which was being unlocked, as my name was shouted out loudly.

I came out following the policeman. There, at the big counter, was a friend waiting. It was Andrew Lukhele, an advocate who was also a good friend and an Alexandra resident. He had managed to negotiate a trespass fine and I was free.

Outside waiting in his car was dear Yolisa.

I was impressed that her escape was not only to save herself, but to seek and find help to get me out of jail. Our friendship continues to thrive and I still rely on her for cool-headed, practical solutions.

At this time, marriage was furthest from my mind. I was still looking forward to entering university and, with Uncle Kenny's encouragement, had applied to what was then Pius XII University, at Roma Mission in Lesotho. When I had refused to go to the Bantustan Turfloop University, 1961 became a gap year for me. The sexual terrorism I had experienced in Alexandra as a very young teenager, the train journey to Inanda Seminary with testosterone-charged young men on the rampage in the train corridors, the lustful conduct of close male friends as soon as you were alone with them, the bold remarks about one's physical attributes, and more, did not make for a keen interest in a relationship. There was something that turned men beastly about sex and it did not assist in one's own self-regard. Additionally, coming from Inanda, the idea of men in charge, of men casually treating women as children they could rebuke – even punish and control – had become anathema, even as it was a common occurrence in society.

One of my closest friends in this time was Mokgadi Tlakula. She is Uncle Bigvai's daughter. We were born in the same year, the two Masekela girls at Roma in 1962. Even in the rarefied air of university life there were tsotsi-minded bullies who preyed on women. Our excitement at being the first Masekela women to enter university was soon deflated A male student called Herman stalked my cousin, threatening us with violence as he tried to coerce Mokgadi into having a relationship with him. It was like the return to the knife-wielding thugs who made the life of all women in the townships an outrage. It was the intervention of Alfred Moleah (who later became the vice chancellor of the University of Transkei and South African ambassador to Vienna), another Johannesburg student, that helped to ease the situation, although the threat of violence continued to rear its head whenever Herman felt like exercising his brute force.

One of the first people I wrote to was Nat. I had been struck by the rugged mountains framing the background to the school. Having seen the spectacular green valleys on the train journey to Durban, and the undulating hills rising and falling on the meandering railroad track, in and out of what seemed to be endless tunnels, the landscape from Maseru, the capital of Lesotho, out to Roma was a stunning contrast. Rocky ridges grinning from the ground were visible from the car as we approached the environs of the college, and though I had known dongas in the eroded streets of Alexandra this blatantly craggy landscape was an assault on my senses. It was as if the earth had bared its teeth and was ready to swallow up every bit of green growth; the evidence of stolen soil, carried away to the rich land of South Africa by rain, was every-where. It was mind-boggling how the discriminatory policies of South African settlers throughout the long decades seemed to have harnessed nature, so that almost all the wealth was owned by the minority in South Africa. Taking a walk outside the university was like a entering a science fiction landscape, all bare and arid with stubborn tufts of grass flaring out here and there.

One of the English literature professors was a Father Tuohy from Ireland, and I immediately established an affection for him because he was a sensitive interpreter of the human emotions in English texts. He became my favourite and ultimately he gave me strong support when one of the American Fulbright scholars, who was an exchange fellow, became enamoured of me. It was a pure courtship, almost chaste, and innocent. We laughed a lot and spent our free time visiting Maseru, talking about African literature, the political situation in South Africa and his very con-servative Pennsylvania Dutch family who would not approve of our friendship.

I felt safe with Peter and I liked it that he was not after my body and that we discussed books and politics, just as in the novels I had read about young British ladies on horses or taking walks alone in the countryside where they encountered reluctant suitors. Our courtship was also constrained by the parochialism of the small intellectual and religious community at Roma. We were looking forward to getting married, and having the free-dom to express ourselves in Ghana – Peter was to leave for Legon University to complete his exchange year there, at the School for African Studies, where renowned scholars like W.E.B. Du Bois and the great African musicologist Nana Nketia were fellows.

During the presidency of Kwame Nkrumah some of the greatest artists and politicians from the continent and the African diaspora gravitated towards Accra, which had become the leading centre of learning and culture under the leadership of a radical, urbane president who expressed ambitious revolutionary ideas not only for Ghana but for pan-Africanists all over the world.

It was my first encounter with the notion of African literature, having first been seduced in high school by the enthusiastic explication of the Wordsworth poem about daffodils. It was from Peter's bookcase that I first read *Things Fall Apart* by Chinua Achebe. Raised primarily in urban areas and with a strong multi-ethnic family background, I had not been exposed to the so-called oral tradition of African literature. It was only at Inanda that I began to understand the incompleteness of my education. There, it was compulsory to study isiZulu. In time, the formal study of Zulu language and literature became my favourite subject. I passed matric with very poor results, but my highest marks were in isiZulu.

Whatever storytelling I experienced as a child was incidental, and not woven into my everyday life. No one ever sat me down to memorise and understand the origins of my family name, and I picked up the narrative of the Masekela genealogy much later in life, in my late adulthood, in particular when my brother was writing his memoir, *Still Grazing*. He spent many weeks in Limpopo getting instruction from our cousin Ramapolo Ramokgopa about the saga of the Masekelas. Hugh adored Ramapolo, his namesake, in part because Ramapolo was also a famous actor in his time. He was a leading actor in a long-running TV series called *Bophelo ke Semphekgo* during the Bantustan era. Hugh loved all artists and he was proud of being the genealogy student of a cousin who was a star.

In Setlokwa, '*sekela*' means going around, finding a way, a road.

I named my youngest son Selema, after my grandfather, and the full name Selematsila actually means 'cultivator of the road'. In the I-know-better manner of a loving elder brother, Hugh told me over and over again how the Masekelas were foreigners in Limpopo and that they were originally from a neighbouring country. It was unclear whether my paternal forebears came from Botswana, Zimbabwe or the Congo. At any rate, they had forged a path through the wilds and finally landed in Botlokwa, where eventually my grandfather had married the daughter of the great Chief Ramokgopa.

But I digress. Hugh looms large, glaring, bright, blaring his trumpet loud, taking centre stage, and this is about me. It is about how, in later years, my aesthetic choices were shaped by the Anglo-Saxon impulse. At school it was Shakespeare, Wordsworth, Shelley, Kipling and the like. Though I had no clue about the physical appearance of a daffodil, the performances by my successive teachers about this yellow English flower were virtuoso renderings that engraved the yellow field forever in my mind. There was little in the scrappy, dusty life of the townships that could compare to the Edenic scenes of English literature. The reserves were hardly pastoral.

I could only imagine my future inhabited by lots of books. I leaned towards the life of the mind, and my father's lessons in observing the minutiae of the physical world inspired the form of my imagination. This is all to say that it was ironic that it was meeting Peter Knauss that radicalised my perspective of African history and culture. His bookcase at Roma sparkled with the orange paperbacks from the Heinemann African Writers Series. Heinemann published Chinua Achebe's *Things Fall Apart* in 1958 and it became a world classic. Like many North Americans and Europeans, Peter was in the post-independence flock of young scholars who got grants from university foundations to study Africa at the source. A number of radical scholars from colonial institutions, from the African diaspora and from leading universities world-wide were employed in the post-independent African studies departments on the continent; Makerere in Uganda and Ibadan in Nigeria were among the leading institutions that attracted expatri-ate students. Kwame Nkrumah became the foremost promoter of African scholarship, and gathered scholars from the world's leading institutions to work at Legon University. Among them were Thomas Hodgkin, who founded the Institute of African Studies in 1962, where Peter was among the international research students.

❖ ❖ ❖

GHANA BECAME a haven for freedom fighters. It is where I met the fabulous Maya Angelou, the African-American singer, actor, dancer, poet, political activist, feminist and renowned memoirist. I was a young, confused twenty-two-year-old, momentarily lost abroad.

I left South Africa on 7 February 1963 on an exit permit, full of dreams about continuing my education and pursuing the fight for freedom with the support of the man who loved me. I had been denied a passport and most of the people I had come to admire and respect were suffering from persecution on all sides, in jail or under house arrest, or had been banished, listed and named. For the rest, it was the daily challenge of keeping the home fires burning in the knowledge of the absent ones suffering torture, hunger and relentless brutality.

By then, the Security Branch had almost broken the back of the liberation movement.

I flew to Accra via Lagos on a British Overseas Air Cor-poration (BOAC) flight and in the air there was no apartheid. I had never been on a plane before but the anticipation of seeing

Peter again outweighed everything else. We were not allowed to disembark at the airport in Lagos, where the plane was scheduled to stop. It was just as well: the hot thick air from outside soon enveloped us and was worse than any humidity I had felt at Inanda. I had a mild foreboding about the next stop in Accra. I could not see clearly from my aisle seat, but I noticed that there was not a single white face among the uniformed airport staff who were receiving the arriving passengers. The booming voice over the public address system was also distinctly different from any accent I had ever heard in South Africa. Only when I listened more attentively could I tell that it was English. I could not believe that an African person had the authority to make an announcement in a plane at an airport.

I did not even feel the hot weather when we finally landed in Accra. I had never seen so many black people in charge of any public facility in my life. There was no white supervisor and all the officials were calmly going about their business. I was the odd one out, marvelling at what was ordinary.

Then I saw Peter.

My new life in Ghana was about to begin.

ACKNOWLEDGEMENTS

I COULD write a book filled with the names of all the people who made this book possible, but the only one who inspired it is my ouma, Johanna Mabena Bower, 1887–1991.

I honour her and all the grandmothers who survived the South African wars, unsung.

I thank Gail Berman for introducing me to the work of Professor Peter Delius, which opened the world into the terrors of Johanna's childhood. Conquest was not conversation.

My gratitude also to Max and Mokgadi Tlakula, Lindiwe Mabuza, and Vincent Mai and Mary Metcalfe, who read the early snippets and gave me the courage and support to keep on writing.

I am especially grateful to my many young friends who raise the feminist bar for me.

Fond thanks to my thoughtful editor, Angela Voges, who valued every word, patiently gathered all the fragments and joined them together, piece by piece, to sew this quilt.

Above all, thank you to Jonathan Ball Publishers, especially Nkanyezi Tshabalala, whose faith in me and active interest pushed me to the finish.

Books

Abrahams, P. 1950. *Wild Conquest: A Novel of the Great Trek in South Africa*. New York, NY: Harper & Brothers.

Delius, P. 2017. *The Land Belongs to Us.* Johannesburg: Ravan Press.

Dlamini, J. 2009. *Native Nostalgia.* Johannesburg: Jacana Media.

Dubow, S. & Jeeves, A. (eds). 2005. *South Africa's 1940s: Worlds of Possibilities.* Cape Town: Double Storey Books.

Masekela, H. & Cheers, M. 2015. *Still Grazing: The Musical Journey of Hugh Masekela.* Johannesburg: Jacana Media.

Mathiane, N. 2016. *Eyes in the Night: An Untold Zulu Story.* Johannesburg: Bookstorm.

Mhlongo, N. (ed.). 2019. *Black Tax: Burden or Ubuntu?* Johannesburg: Jonathan Ball Publishers.

Miles, E. 1993. *Artists' Birthday Calendar.* Johannesburg: FUBA Academy.

Miles, E. 1997. *Land and Lives: A Story of Early Black Artists.* Cape Town: Human & Rousseau.

Mokgokong, S. 2016. *Kolobe: I Led A Full Life – An Autobiography.* South Africa: Business Print.

Olusoga, D. 2014. *The World's War.* London: Head of Zeus Ltd.

Plaatjie, T.S. 2007. *Native Life in South Africa* (third edition). Johannesburg: Picador Africa.

Tema, B. 2005. *The People of Welgeval.* Cape Town: Zebra Press.

Reports

South African Institute of Race Relations. 1937. *Talitha Home for Non-European Girls: Report for 1935 to 1937*. South African Institute of Race Relations (SAIRR) 1892–1974 collection. Johannesburg: Historical Papers Research Archive.

South African Institute of Race Relations. 1951. *Entokozweni: First Report 1st January to 31st December, 1951*. South African Institute of Race Relations (SAIRR) 1892–1974 collection. Johannesburg: Historical Papers Research Archive.

South African Institute of Race Relations. 1960. *National Council of African Women: 1960 General Secretary's Report*. South African Institute of Race Relations (SAIRR) 1892–1974 collection. Johannesburg: Historical Papers Research Archive.

Journal articles

Delius, P. 2010. Recapturing Captives and Conversations with 'Cannibals': In Pursuit of a Neglected Stratum in South African History. *Journal of Southern African Studies* 36(1): 7–23.

Marks, S. 2000. Changing history, changing histories: Separations and connections in the lives of South African women. *Journal of African Cultural Studies* 13(1): 94–106.

Nauright, J. 1998. 'The Mecca of Native Scum' and 'a running sore of evil': White Johannesburg and the Alexandra Township removal debate, 1935–1945. *Kleio* 30(1): 64–88.

Nkomo, S.N. 2012. Looking for Maria, her sisters, daughters and sons. *International Journal of African Renaissance Studies* 7(2): 96–107.

Pakendorf, G. 1997. 'For there is no power but of God': The Berlin Mission and the challenges of colonial South Africa. *Missionalia* 25(3): 255–273.

Magazine articles

Gribble, J. 2008. The *SS Mendi*: A forgotten story of prejudice and loss. *British Archaeology* 99, March/April 2008, pp. 17–21.

Websites

Brand South Africa. 2006. Remembering the *SS Mendi*. *Brand South Africa*, 3 October 2006. Available at https://www. brandsouthafrica.com/people-culture/history-heritage/ remembering-the-ss-mendi (accessed 21 June 2021).

Heese, H.F. 2005. The Berlin Mission Society and Black Europeans: The Cases of Klaus Kuhn, Jan Sekoto and Gerard Sekoto. Black European Studies Database. Available at http://www.best.uni-mainz.de/modules/AMS/article.php?storyid=82 (accessed 21 June 2021).

Honikman, M. 2017. Memories of black South African soldiers who bore arms and fought in War II. *Mail & Guardian*, 14 March 2017. Available at https://mg.co.za/article/2017-03-14-memories-of-black-south-african-soldiers-who-bore-arms-and-fought-in-war-ii (accessed 13 April 2019).

Koen, G. 2016. Our history … in ruins. *City Press*, 11 July 2016. Available at https://city-press.news24.com/Trending/our-historyin-ruins-20160711 (accessed 30 July 2019).

Krydz Ikwuemesi, C. 2018. An Artist's Diary II: The Long Road to Abidjan. *Fortunate Traveller*, 2 March 2018. Available at https:// www.fortunatetraveller.com/an-artists-diary-ii-the-long-road-to-abidjan-by-c-krydz-ikwuemesi/ (accessed 25 March 2019).

Mzamane, M.V. 2007. Drilling the death drill on a sinking ship. *Sunday Times* Heritage Project. Available at http://sthp.saha.org. za/memorial/articles/drilling_the_death_drill_on_a_sinking_ship.htm (accessed 21 June 2021).

SA Venues. (n.d.). Botshabelo Mission Station. Available at https:// www.sa-venues.com/attractionsmpl/botshabelo-mission-station. php (accessed 21 June 2021).

Smith, A. 2007. They died like warriors: Tale of the *SS Mendi*. *Independent*, 21 July 2007. Available at https://www.independent. co.uk/news/uk/this-britain/they-died-like-warriors-tale-of-the-ss-mendi-5334107.html (accessed 21 June 2021).

South African History Online. (n.d.). Daniel Francois Malan. Available at https://www.sahistory.org.za/people/daniel-francois-malan (accessed 3 December 2019).

South African History Online. (n.d.). European Missionaries in Southern Africa: The Role of the Missionaries. Available at https://www.sahistory.org.za/article/european-missionaries-southern-africa-role-missionaries (accessed 23 February 2019).

South African History Online. (n.d.). General South African History Timeline: 1960s. Available at https://www.sahistory.org.za/ article/general-south-african-history-timeline-1960s (accessed 21 June 2021).

South African History Online. (n.d.). General South African History Timeline: 1950s. Available from https://www.sahistory.org.za/ article/general-south-african-history-timeline-1950s (accessed 21 June 2021).

South African History Online. Liberation history Timeline 1940– 1949. Available from https://www.sahistory.org.za/article/ liberation-history-timeline-1940-1949 (accessed 18 October 2019).

Wessex Archaeology. 2008. Wreck of the *SS Mendi*. 5 January 2008. Available at https://www.wessexarch.co.uk/our-work/wreck-ss-mendi (accessed 21 June 2021).

Wikipedia. (n.d.). John Wesley College. Available at https:// en.wikipedia.org/wiki/John_Wesley_College (accessed 21 June 2021).

Poem

De Andrade, M. 2016. 'The Valuable Time of Maturity'. Available at https://www.poemhunter.com/poem/the-valuable-time-of-maturity/ (accessed 5 January 2019).

Papers

Alexander, P. 2008. *Culture and conflicts: Witbank colliery life, 1900–1950*. PhD thesis, Centre for Sociological Research, University of Johannesburg.

Delius, P. 1987. The Ndzundza Ndebele: Indenture and the making of Ethnic Identity, 1883–1914. Paper presented at the Wits History Workshop: The Making of Class, 9–14 February 1987. Johannesburg: University of the Witwatersrand.

Morrel, R. 1987. 'Pipping a little game in the bud' – Pixley Isaka ka Seme, land purchase and rural differentiation in the Eastern Transvaal. Paper presented at the Wits History Workshop: The Making of Class, 9–14 February 1987. Johannesburg: University of the Witwatersrand.